JOHN D. ROCKEFELLER
Oil Baron and Philanthropist

JOHN D. ROCKEFELLER
Oil Baron and Philanthropist

Rosemary Laughlin

620 South Elm Street, Suite 384
Greensboro, North Carolina 27406
http://www.morganreynolds.com

JOHN D. ROCKEFELLER: OIL BARON AND PHILANTHROPIST

Copyright © 2001 by Rosemary Laughlin

*Picture credits: Courtesy of the Rockefeller Archive Center
and the Library of Congress*

Library of Congress Cataloging-in-Publication Data

Laughlin, Rosemary.
    John D. Rockefeller : oil baron and philanthropist / Rosemary Laughlin.
        p. cm.
    Includes bibliographical references and index.
    ISBN 1-883846-59-5 (lib. bdg.)
    1. Rockefeller, John D. (John Davison), 1839-1937--Juvenile literature. 2. Capitalists
and financiers--United States--Biography--Juvenile literature. 3. Industrialists--United
States--Biography--Juvenile literature. 4. Philanthropists--United
States--Biography--Juvenile literature. [1. Rockefeller, John D. (John Davison),
1839-1937. 2. Capitalists and financiers. 3. Millionaires. 4. Philanthropists.] I. Title.

CT275.R75 .L34 2001
338.7'62233882'092--dc21
    [B]

                                                                    00-052712

Printed in the United States of America
First Edition

Contents

John D. Rockefeller
(Courtesy of the Rockefeller Archive Center.)

Chapter One

Family History

Thousands of years ago, in the wooded hills of north-western Pennsylvania, a black, thick liquid began to ooze to the surface. It bubbled up through the soil and left black scum floating on the tops of creeks. When the Seneca Indians migrated into the area, they used the substance as a medicine to soothe coughs and sore muscles and to help heal wounds. When Europeans came to the area in the seventeenth and eighteenth centuries as fur traders and colonists, they learned about the oil from the Native Americans. The Europeans called the substance "rock oil," to distinguish it from animal fat and plant oils.

By the mid-1800s, rock oil had become one of the "cure-alls" peddled by the patent medicine salesmen who traveled the lanes and byways to the small towns and frontier farms. It may even have been sold by William Avery Rockefeller, one of the most colorful and outrageous "docs" to travel the Northeast and Midwest. Bill Rockefeller was willing to say just about anything to make a quick sale. He fit the definition of *flim-flam man*, *huckster, quack,* and *mountebank.* He was also the father of John D. Rockefeller, who would become one of America's most influential businessmen and the world's richest man.

The name *Rockefeller* is the German version of the original French *Roquefeuille.* The Protestant family left France for Koblenz, Germany, after the Catholic King Louis XIV renounced his policy of religious tolerance in 1685. In the 1700s, various Rockefellers moved across the Atlantic to settle as farmers in New Jersey and New York.

William Avery Rockefeller, born in 1810, hated physical labor from his childhood. As a teen, he went off on peddling trips when he felt like it, even disappearing when the family moved. He sold trinkets and kaleidoscope viewers. He exaggerated the benefits of home-brewed remedies and sold drugstore medicines at inflated prices. He sometimes pretended to be deaf and dumb in order to get people to talk unguardedly. He was also tall, well built, and handsome enough to attract the attentions of the ladies, including the red-haired, blue-eyed Eliza Davison.

Eliza Davison could scarcely have been more unlike "Big Bill" Rockefeller. After her mother's death, she was raised by her father and an older sister. They were thrifty, self-disciplined, no-nonsense Scotch-Irish who had converted to the Baptist faith. Her father feared that Eliza's new suitor, William Avery, was after his money and farm.

William Avery Rockefeller
*(Courtesy of the Rockefeller
Archive Center.)*

Eliza Davison Rockefeller
*(Courtesy of the Rockefeller
Archive Center.)*

There must have been a rebellious streak somewhere in Eliza because she went against her father's wishes and married "Big Bill." Twenty-four years old at the time of her wedding, Eliza soon regretted not listening to her father. During her marriage she had six children, moved from town to town, and learned to adjust to the frequent disappearances of her husband, who was gone much of the time. Through all the trials of being married to "Big Bill," Eliza Davison Rockefeller remained loyal to her wandering husband and maintained a firm dignity before her children and the community.

When Big Bill returned to his family after his extended trips, he was always well-dressed, usually loaded with money, and filled with hearty jokes and tales. Big Bill was an entertainer by nature, almost like a hero from a frontier tall-tale. The word for his lifestyle was *big* when he was home. So was his talk. When he was gone, his deeds and his whereabouts were a mystery.

John Davison Rockefeller was the second child and the oldest boy born to Bill and Eliza. He and his older sister Lucy were followed by William, Mary Ann, and the twins: Frank and Frances. Little Frances died at two years old. John was born in the small farmhouse near Richford, New York, but the family moved to a much larger and more pleasant home outside Moravia on the shores of Lake Owasco. Later, John recalled these as happy days. Big Bill stayed around long enough to start a logging business, stock the lake with fish, and help start a school.

From left to right: John, Lucy, Mary Ann, Frank, and William.
(Courtesy of the Rockefeller Archive Center.)

He hired a man to help with the farm work. For once, he seemed to cherish stability.

In photographs taken of the Rockefeller family, young John appears solemn, but his face also hints at the slow and reflective method that he applied to everything he did, even the games he played. When opponents at checkers or chess complained about the length of time between his moves, he would reply quietly, "You don't think I'm playing to get beaten, do you?"

Her Baptist faith was a great source of spiritual and emotional support for Eliza. She read the Bible and took her family to church. Young John witnessed the faith in his mother and found that he, too, received guidance and strength from Baptist beliefs and practices.

These Baptists renounced drinking, smoking, dancing, card-playing, and theater-going. They did *not* hold to the old Calvinist belief in predestination, that is, that only certain people—called the Elect—had already been chosen by God to be saved for an afterlife in Heaven. They believed that anybody who chose the path of Jesus Christ and lived righteously would be saved. In other words, spiritual destiny was in one's own hands. Egalitarianism was also reflected in the Northern Baptists' decision in 1845 that slavery was wrong. They became abolitionists who worked to end slavery. Some even helped with the Underground Railroad. From an early age, John D. Rockefeller was aware of a major social concern beyond his own family's welfare.

It was not only his attraction to a strict religion that made Rockefeller serious. His mother's reliance on him when Big Bill was on the road—she never knew where he was or when he would return—gave John a strong sense of duty and responsibility. Eliza Rockefeller always showed her pride and confidence in her oldest son. Big Bill might amaze the neighborhood with his ventriloquism, his sharpshooting, and his fiddle-playing, but John was the stalwart wood-chopper, account keeper, and churchgoer.

From his mother, John learned to be prudent and reflective before making decisions. "We will let it simmer," was her way of expressing how she approached difficult decisions. This was a skill he would use all his business life. Eliza was a strict disciplinarian and did not hesitate to reinforce her lessons in prudence and obedience with a birch switch.

In 1849, the Rockefellers moved to near Owego, New York, about thirty miles from Moravia. Big Bill may have chosen Owego because of better lumber possibilities or because patent medicine "docs" liked to gather there. Here, John D. Rockefeller attended an excellent secondary school, Owego Academy, where he learned to write essays and give speeches. He was not an outstanding student, though he was very good at math. He himself said, "I was not an easy student, and I had to apply myself diligently to my lessons." He was intrigued by the new technologies the principal demonstrated for the students, such as the telegraph and the galvanic battery.

In 1853, Big Bill uprooted Eliza and the children once again. They found themselves on the train bound for Strongsville, Ohio, a town near Cleveland. Big Bill lodged Eliza and the children with his sister's family in a small house. The move was humiliating, as well as uncomfortable. Big Bill listed himself in the Cleveland directory as a "botanic physician" and promptly went out on the road. The move put him closer to less-settled country where it was easier to find desperate, isolated people who suffered aches, pains, and diseases.

Not long after the family settled in their new home, a Strongsville neighbor happened to be visiting a small town where he saw the sign: "Dr. William A. Rockefeller, the Celebrated Cancer Specialist, Here for One Day Only. All cases of cancer cured unless too far gone and then can be greatly benefitted." The neighbor listened while Big Bill delivered his spiel and sold his bottled cures for as much as twenty-five dollars. The neighbor reported his discovery, and everybody in Strongsville began calling Big Bill "Doc Rockefeller." Big Bill enjoyed the exposé, but the family did not.

At fifteen years old, John was humiliated when he was told he had to study for one term in an elementary school before he could enter the secondary school in Cleveland. Big Bill saw to it that John and his brother Bill were settled in a boarding house closer to the school. As in Owego, John was serious about his studies. He was superb with numbers. One thing Big Bill stressed was the importance of keeping account of every penny.

Big Bill loved money. In 1855, he began to need more of it when, under the name of Dr. William Levingstone, he married another, much younger, woman in Nichols, New York. For years, Big Bill traveled back and forth between the two families, keeping each a secret from the other. Eliza did not know that her husband was a bigamist.

Two months before his high school graduation, John received a letter from Big Bill telling him to drop his college plans and to prepare himself for business. Big Bill was worried about money. He needed his oldest son to contribute to the household.

John obeyed his father and signed up for a three-month

business course at E.G. Folsom's Commercial College in Cleveland. He learned double-entry bookkeeping, which taught him how to keep track of both expenses and earnings. He also learned the basics of business law and banking. He practiced penmanship so that his ledger entries would be legible. John was still sixteen when he finished school and was ready to find work. If he was disappointed that his formal education was ending, he never admitted it. Years later he said only that, "There were younger brothers and sisters to educate, and it seemed wise for me to go into business." Because of his father's selfishness and deceit, he had to sacrifice an official high school diploma and graduation with his classmates. The piano playing he had once loved to practice was a distant memory. He wanted to be of help to his mother, and he never wanted to be dependent on his father again. So after three months in a business course, reliable John D. Rockefeller set out to find a job.

Rockefeller later described his first job search: "I was working every day at my business—the business of looking for work." It was not easy in the summer of 1855. There had been a nationwide recession in the early part of the decade and economic times were still not good in Cleveland. Determined, Rockefeller used the city directory to identify which businesses had the best financial reputations. "I went to the railroads, to the banks, to the wholesale merchants," he said. "I did not go to any small establishments. I did not guess what it would be, but I was after something big." At each business he would ask to speak to the head person. To whomever would see him he would say, "I understand bookkeeping, and I'd like to get work."

For six weeks, Monday through Saturday, young Rockefeller methodically walked the hot streets, dressed neatly in suit, high collar, and tie. "No one wanted a boy, and very few showed any overwhelming anxiety to talk to me on the subject," he said later. But he refused to be discouraged and often returned to the same businesses several times.

As Rockefeller walked the city streets, he noted many things about Cleveland, a new city of 25,000 people. Linked to the Ohio River by a canal opened in 1830, new immigrants poured into the port city located on the southeast shore of Lake Erie. It was also close enough to the western terminus of the Erie Canal to participate in the profitable trade with New York and New England. Iron ore, salt, corn, and grain came in on barges and by rail from the west; coal came from the east. Rail and water transports met and connected, transferring freight from boat to rail and back. Rockefeller entered his working life just as the agrarian economy of the Midwest was making the transition to an industrial economy. On the horizon were unparalleled opportunities for businessmen created by new technologies, such as steelmaking, communications, energy, and refrigeration.

All his long life, Rockefeller would remember and

celebrate September 26 as though it were a birthday. On this day in 1855, the produce shipping and warehouse company of Hewitt & Tuttle gave him a job. After an interview with both the junior and senior partners and a test of his handwriting for legibility, he was told to take off his coat and to begin work immediately as an assistant bookkeeper. Salary was not mentioned. Since unpaid apprenticeships were common, Rockefeller was unsure what to expect. He knew he could not afford to keep the job if it were unpaid, but he came to work every day, diligently learning new skills. He did not receive his first paycheck until three months later.

Chapter Two

Smart Young Businessman

Rockefeller loved his bookkeeper's job at Hewitt & Tuttle. Instead of viewing it as a long, tedious day of bookkeeping in exchange for wages, he saw it as a chance to learn "all the method and system of the office." The numbers he added and subtracted in his columns of debits and credits represented the key to success and profit. Numbers were rational and helped the businessman to make logical, unemotional decisions. In addition to keeping the books, Rockefeller also had to collect money when bills or rents went unpaid. Though he did not enjoy it, he set about this task with characteristic tenacity.

Since Hewitt & Tuttle dealt with more than one product, Rockefeller learned a system of bookkeeping that involved many items and different modes for transporting them. He had to calculate, often by mental arithmetic, the best shipping mode—either rail, ship, or canal. He had to factor in possible damage or delays. He made frequent use of the newest communication technology: the telegraph. Every day, he was caught up in his work. As he put it, "The zest of the work is maintained by something better than the mere accumulation of money."

Outside of work, Rockefeller was finding both spiritual and social nurturing at the Erie Street Baptist Mission Church. His brother William attended with him. In 1854, Rockefeller made his profession of faith and was baptized by full immersion. He soon began his long career as a Sunday school teacher, and he also did janitorial chores for the church, such as sweeping floors, cleaning lamps, and building the fire for warmth in winter.

In 1856, after John was beginning to make a success at Hewitt & Tuttle, Big Bill came back into town. He ordered his oldest son to build a house in Cleveland for Eliza and the children. He said he wanted John to oversee the construction to learn self-reliance and gain experience. The dutiful son, who already had his full-time job as well as his church duties, did not hesitate. He undertook all the details of having a house constructed, such as soliciting bids and dealing with inspections. Then, as the house neared completion, Big Bill demanded that John pay rent to live in it! There is no record of John protesting this decision.

By 1859, Rockefeller was growing restless at his job. John thought he was underpaid at Hewitt & Tuttle. He asked for a raise and was turned down. Within days he had formed a partnership with a former classmate from commercial college, Maurice B. Clark. The two young entrepreneurs proposed to buy and sell farm products such as grain, hay, and meat and to arrange for shipping to distant markets.

To start his new business, Rockefeller borrowed $1000 from Big Bill, who charged his son ten percent interest, even though prevailing rates were much lower. This was true to form: Big Bill often boasted of teaching his sons the hard truths of making money, including not trusting family or associates more than strangers in deals. If the high interest rate angered John, he never showed it.

Rockefeller did have some anger at another development. When a third partner, George Gardner, the son of a prominent family, was invited to join the fledgling firm in order to strengthen it financially, *Rockefeller* was dropped from the company's name and replaced with *Gardner*. His partners felt that the Gardner name stood for security in Cleveland, while no one knew who Rockefeller was.

The firm of Clark, Gardner and Company was launched on March 18, 1859, and was a success from the beginning. It operated at 32 River Street. Rockefeller's share of the new company's first year profits of $4400 was almost three times his salary at Hewitt & Tuttle.

From the beginning, however, there were problems at the new firm. Rockefeller disapproved of George Gardner's love of personal extravagances. What Rockefeller thought excess, such as a $2000 yacht, Gardner thought of as the necessary implements that made life worth living. Rockefeller thought such extravagances would ruin their reputation with the bankers. He knew they would need access to large amounts of cash at critical times. For two years, tensions grew in the firm until in 1862 Rockefeller was able to cut Gardner out of the business and restore the name Clark & Rockefeller.

In fact, it *was* Rockefeller's staid behavior, consistency, honesty, and conservative business practices, as well as his involvement in the Erie Street Baptist Mission Church, that made bankers willing to give the firm loans. When Rockefeller had to travel to increase trade, he proved to be a very good salesman because of his direct, dignified approach. Years later, he remembered his sale's pitch:

> 'We are engaged in business,' I would say. 'You may already have a commission house that is quite satisfactory to you. If so, I am not seeking your trade—I just want you to know about us. We are prepared to do business, we hope we can do it as well as anybody else . . . and if you make a change, won't you kindly give us young men a chance?' . . . I found that old men had confidence in me right away . . . and the consignments came in and our business was increased and it opened up a new world for me.

A ready supply of cash was critical to the success of the warehouse. It was important that the bankers trusted a customer's honesty and had faith that he used sound business principles. One banker decided to test Rockefeller. He had a customer come into the offices of Clark & Rockefeller promising huge profits if he could receive payment for produce before it arrived. He was offering larger profits if Rockefeller broke one of his rules of never paying for produce before it was in his warehouse. The man did not even have proof that the produce was en route to the firm's warehouse. When Rockefeller denied his request, the man began to rant and rave.

Despite this pressure, Rockefeller did not give in. However, he tried very hard to placate the man and keep him as a customer. Because the fake customer played his role to the very end, Rockefeller watched him walk away, convinced that he had lost his business. Later, he found out that he had passed the test and proven himself as a fiscally sound businessman. He had solidified his good reputation and continued to receive the loans he needed at good terms.

Rockefeller also helped himself by preparing beforehand before asking for loans. He would inquire for advice at various banks about investing at least twice the amount he actually wanted to borrow. Thus, the perception in the business community was that he had lots of money, and the banker who eventually got his loan request would not be worried that Rockefeller was without *collateral* (something valuable that can be given to the loaner, if the borrower cannot pay back).

When the Civil War began in April 1861, Rockefeller was sympathetic to the North. He was an abolitionist, had contributed money to the Underground Railroad, and had voted for Abraham Lincoln. He said later that he wanted to answer the call for volunteers, but because he was the head of his family and was involved in a new business that needed him, he was simply unable to leave Cleveland. The law allowed a man to hire a substitute for $300 if he were the sole support of his family. Rockefeller paid for a substitute and contributed additional money to the war effort.

The war was a terrible experience for the United States, but in the North it spurred the growth of industrialization. New railroads were built to haul goods and troops. Coal and iron ore were mined to build weapons and to fuel ships and trains. Factories sprung up to process food and produce clothing, arms, and transportation for the soldiers. When the war ended in 1865, veterans and workers returned home wanting to have more and better things in life.

Chapter Three

The New Oil Industry

In 1848, gold had been discovered in California and a wave of gold-seekers rushed into the state. The gold hunters were quickly followed by men and women eager to make money selling goods and services to the gold miners. A decade later, the same thing happened in Pennsylvania, except this time the earth was rendering up oil.

Although for centuries candles made from tallow or beeswax had been the primary means of illumination, by the 1850s new methods of pushing back the night had come into use. Oil lanterns and lamps using extended wicks that allowed the oil to burn slowly were common in most homes. The fuel that provided the best bright, steady light was whale oil, but it became increasingly expensive as the herds off the Atlantic coast had been over hunted and the whalers were forced to sail into the South Pacific. These voyages could last up to three years. There were coal oils, animal oils, and plant oils that could be used in lamps, but they were neither as bright nor as stable. They also tended to clog. It was a common occurrence for lamp explosions to set homes on fire.

In 1853, a Classics scholar and school superintendent named George Bissell was visiting Dartmouth, his former college. In a professor's office he noticed a bottle of Pennsylvania rock oil. He had just passed through northwestern Pennsylvania, the region from which it came, and had seen people scooping it from the ground or soaking it up with rags in order to sell it as a "patent" medicine. Bissell knew that the rock oil was flammable, and he had a sudden insight that it might be the source of good, cheap light. He hired a Yale University chemist, Benjamin Silliman, Jr., to test his theory.

There was no question that rock oil was flammable. The question was, could it be distilled in a simple, inexpensive way that would provide a low cost and stable illuminating oil? Silliman's analysis showed that Pennsylvania rock oil could be boiled at different temperatures, yielding varied products. One of these was a high quality illumination oil and another was a lubricant. Silliman knew the machines being invented for factories and transportation needed oil to restrict friction among moving parts. Bissell had found two needed products that could be refined from the rock oil and set out to find investors for his Pennsylvania Rock Oil Company.

Bissell soon discovered that a process to extract *kerosene*, or parrafin oil, from coal had already been developed in Europe, where a lamp with a glass chimney that prevented smoke and odor from escaping had also been invented. There were even kerosene production plants in New York and Boston. Bissell's first challenge was to find out how much rock oil, or *petroleum*, there was in Pennsylvania. To do this he would have to find a different method of extraction than the skimming, digging, and rag-dipping used by the medicine hucksters.

Bissell had his next insight when he went into a drug store one hot day to cool off. He saw an advertisement with a picture of *derricks*, machines used to bore into the earth, used for salt drilling. If you could drill for salt, why couldn't you drill for petroleum?

In 1857, Bissell hired a jack-of-all trades named Edwin Drake to buy some land and start drilling near Titusville, Pennsylvania. Most of Drake's employees working the drill soon thought his project was crazy and quit. But Drake was personally committed and, after getting more money from Bissell's new Seneca Oil Company, he hired a blacksmith to build a steam engine that would power the drill.

Over the next months, the investors in Seneca Oil were growing restless. On August 27, 1859, a letter had been mailed instructing Drake to pay his bills and close down. It looked like drilling for oil in Pennsylvania was a flop. Then, near quitting time, the drill hit a gap in the earth at sixty-nine feet and came to rest six inches farther. The next day there was oil in the gap. Drake and the black-smith brought up enough oil with hand pumps to fill every container available. When Drake bought all the whiskey barrels he could find and filled them, the word soon got out that he had struck oil.

Almost overnight the wooded, hilly region was booming. The woods and brush were cleared, and the once leafy, spongy ground was often a muddy quagmire. Ugly equipment and the clanging of pipes and cursing of the workers filled the woods. As in California a decade earlier, the rush to get rich was on.

Just as the first shots of the Civil War were fired at Fort Sumter in South Carolina in April 1861, drillers hit the first real gusher, which yielded 3000 barrels a day. Even more men rushed in to try their luck. In addition to the ramshackle drills, refineries were thrown together to separate the kerosene from the petroleum. The change transformed the area around Titusville and soon the country as a whole. The quality of the Pennsylvania oil and the kerosene that was refined was so high, and the cost so cheap, that other illuminants were soon abandoned. As the war increased the demand for light and for lubricants, there was a ready supply available. Soon there was enough excess oil to provide for a strong foreign export business as well.

The biggest problem was having enough barrels and transportation to get the oil out of the area. The roads were so clogged that one visitor said, "The whole place smells like a corps of soldiers when they have the diarrhea." Gasses released with the oil often ignited and burned entire areas, leaving the landscape hideously blackened. Nothing could stop the rush for wealth, though. When one oil pool dried up, others were found. When there was money to be made, ugliness and mess were of little concern.

Naturally, the western Pennsylvania oil strikes were exciting to the residents of Cleveland, who lived only one day's travel away. Maurice Clark started talking up the wonderful opportunity to Rockefeller. When a chemist friend of Clark's, Samuel Andrews, who worked in a lard-oil refinery, learned how to extract kerosene from crude oil with sulfuric acid, he decided to set up his own kerosene refining business. He turned to his friend Clark and his partner for financing.

The excitement about oil refining coincided with Rockefeller's realization that, in the long run, Cleveland could not compete with Chicago, Milwaukee, and Omaha as a center for grain shipping, meat-packing, and general produce. These cities were closer to the great Midwest prairies and plains, where most of the goods were produced, and would always be able to get the most warehouse business. Rockefeller saw that Cleveland was better suited to be a site for industrial development.

Rockefeller was receptive to Andrews's request for financial backing. Clark then agreed, and the two invested $4000 in the refining business named Andrews, Clark and Company. Rockefeller chose to locate the refinery on a tributary near the Cuyahoga River so that

Edwin Drake (in top hat) stands before the first successful well he drilled in Titusville, Pennsylvania, in 1859.

the refined kerosene could be shipped to Lake Erie and beyond. The refinery could also use the new Atlantic and Great Western Railroad that connected with lines to the Pennsylvania oil fields and on to New York City. Rockefeller was intelligent and foresighted to build near *two* choices of transportation. Ensuring transportation options was one of his most basic principles throughout his business career.

Although Samuel Andrews was placed in charge of the refinery, Rockefeller began spending more and more time at the plant. His instinct and ability to read the numbers convinced him that there was a great deal of money to be made in refining. He also knew that efficiency and thriftiness could result in more profits, and that as the profits began rolling in, it would be more important to remain focused on ways to save and make money. For example, Rockefeller noted that a little sulfuric acid was left after the refining process. Instead of dumping it, he had it converted to fertilizer. Displeased by an error in a plumber's bill, he decided to buy the plant's plumbing materials and hire a company plumber. Later, when demand made the barrels difficult to get, he set up a barrel-making operation. Furthermore, he had the wood dried before it was shipped to the plant. The dried lumber weighed half as much as freshly cut lumber, thus cutting the shipping cost.

Rockefeller's adjustments were not always to the liking of his partner Maurice Clark. Clark disliked what he perceived as extremes in Rockefeller's business behavior. On the one hand, Rockefeller let no detail go unscrutinized. On the other hand, he seemed too willing to borrow money for expansion. It frightened Clark that Rockefeller would risk debt to invest in the refinery. Clark's two vocal brothers agreed with him.

The debt made Clark nervous because he was aware of the increasing competition in the oil industry. There were many other refineries in Cleveland by 1865, and the drying up and discovery of oil in Pennsylvania made for unpredictable boom-bust cycles in which prices could swing widely. In 1861, prices per barrel careened between ten cents and ten dollars! In 1864, they varied between four dollars and twelve dollars. Clark was very cautious, but Rockefeller had faith in the future of oil that was akin to the strength of his Baptist faith. He saw Clark as plodding and shortsighted.

One day when they were arguing about expansion, an angry Clark proposed they dissolve their partnership. Rockefeller surprised him by agreeing and suggested an auction be held so that one would buy the other out. What Clark did not know was that Rockefeller had been preparing for this challenge. He had secretly visited the banks and arranged financing for just such an auction. Almost before he knew it, Clark discovered that what had probably been a challenge made in anger was accepted. In effect, Rockefeller had painstakingly prepared to call his bluff.

The day of the auction the bidding started at $500 and moved up rapidly. When Rockefeller said, "$72,500," Maurice Clark replied, "I'll go no higher, John. The business is yours." Rockefeller was then twenty-five years old. Many years later, he said, "I ever point to that day as the beginning of the success I have made in my life."

As part of the arrangement, Rockefeller gave up his interest in the warehouse business. He had taken the gamble and put his entire future in the oil business. Samuel Andrews remained with the firm and within days the Andrews, Clark and Company sign had been taken down and replaced with one for the newly organized Rockefeller & Andrews Excelsior Oil Works.

As soon as he controlled the refinery, Rockefeller expanded even more, but always with sufficient cash in reserve to keep from being overly reliant on bankers. He bought his own tank cars, warehouses in other cities, and his own boats.

In 1867, Rockefeller met the man who would become his closest associate and friend. The intelligent Henry Morrison Flagler, nine years older, had a religious up-bringing under a Presbyterian minister father. Flagler had been successful in making whiskey but did not like the product. When he shifted to salt manufacture, he got caught in a boom-bust cycle. From this he learned that producers must cooperate, or "unbridled competition" would lead them inevitably to bankruptcy.

John D. Rockefeller and Laura Celestia Spelman were married in 1854.
(Courtesy of the Rockefeller Archive Center.)

When Rockefeller was negotiating a loan from one of Flagler's relatives, Stephen Harkness, the rich Harkness stipulated that as a condition of the loan Flagler be made Rockefeller's treasurer and personal deputy. "Young man," he concluded, "you can have all the money you want . . . I'll make Henry my watch dog."

Soon after joining the firm, Henry Flagler was working in the same office with Rockefeller, and the two men meshed smoothly. Flagler specialized in the transportation of oil and its products. "A friendship founded on business is better than business founded on friendship," Flagler liked to say. He and Rockefeller set out to prevent the business from being shaken by boom-bust occurrences and to make its products the best by controlling efficiency and quality.

A little earlier, Rockefeller had found a wife. Laura Celestia Spelman had been a classmate in his Cleveland high school. She was called Cettie and she became friendly with John, remaining so after he had to leave the school. She sympathetically encouraged him in his 1855 job search. Her family was descended from New England Puritans, who were religious fundamentalists concerned with bettering society. Cettie's father, Harvey Spelman, was a dry-goods merchant who was elected to the Ohio legislature after he worked for a progressive public school system.

The Spelmans were against liquor, dancing, card-playing, and theater. They also opposed slavery and supported equal rights for women. Mr. and Mrs. Spelman would march into saloons and beg the patrons to stop drinking. They also made their home a station on the Underground Railroad. Cettie recalled that if she saw her mother cooking on Sunday, she knew slaves were expected.

Cettie attended Oread, a junior college for women in Worcester, Massachusetts. She taught for several years in the Cleveland public schools. By 1864, John Rockefeller felt he had proven himself adequate to win her consent to marriage. They were perfectly suited in their religious devotion and in their values of duty and thrift. They were married in her parents' house on September 8, 1864. Like many other American couples, they toured Niagara Falls for their honeymoon. Afterwards, they returned home to Cleveland and moved in with John's mother. Six months later, the couple moved into a stately, new house in one of the city's best neighborhoods.

Chapter Four

Standard Oil Company

By 1865, the decade-old oil business was, in Rockefeller's perspective, out of control. As he traveled to the oil patch and looked around Cleveland, he saw a chaos of wells and refiners. The narrow muddy roads and trails leading out of the western Pennsylvania backwoods were clogged with horses and wagons struggling to get oil to the railroad freight stations. Despite the teamsters' work, there seemed to always be more oil to carry, and soon the cost of transporting oil the few miles to the tracks was more than for the trains to carry it to Cleveland or New York. From this situation, the idea of a pipeline to carry the crude to the refineries was born. The first pipelines were wooden, and they had to be built secretly because the teamsters would sabotage them at every opportunity.

It became critical to develop a more sophisticated marketing system as well. At first, buyers rode horseback to individual wells to strike their deals. Eventually, they began meeting with drillers at the hotels in Titusville and

Oil City that seemed to have sprung out of the ground overnight. There were usually three types of transactions: *Spot sales* were immediate exchanges of oil for cash, *regular sales* allowed ten days for completion of the transaction before payment, and *futures* guaranteed a specific quantity of oil delivered on a fixed date at a fixed price.

Soon the trading of futures became a hot item for speculators in Pennsylvania and in distant areas, such as New York, and oil speculation became an American craze. Oil madness lapped out of the oil patch and surrounding cities to the country at large. If the oil producer ran out of oil on the agreed date of a future sale, he had to pay the buyer the difference between the set price and the regular sale price at the time. If the buyer did not come up with the money, he became indebted, which usually meant he had to borrow more—with high interest—to pay off his losses. Some made money in the futures, but many more lost everything.

In many ways, the high-intensity chaos of the oil business was only an extreme version of what was going on in the post-Civil War craze for business and wealth that seemed to start as soon as the last gun was silenced. Soon the names of Cornelius Vanderbilt, Jay Gould, and Collis Huntington were well known, and often hated. The American political system, now firmly controlled by the Republican Party, sided with the businessman. There was little politcal effort made to control the size of the companies that emerged during the so-called Gilded Age. In time, the government began to make efforts to tame the runaway aspects of *laissez-faire* capitalism, but in the decades after the Civil War, "Opportunity!" flashed with allure in people's minds. The "American Dream" came to mean the acquisition of wealth and material possessions. What Rockefeller called "the Great Game" was played with new inventions, newly discovered natural resources, and new methods of organization.

Rockefeller differed from many others of this era by focusing on long-term growth and stability. He always spoke scornfully of get-rich-quick-schemes and had no sympathy for those who lost everything in the pursuit of easy profits. He believed this fast money mind-set was destructive and designed his business to take advantage of those who lacked his wisdom. This ability to concentrate on long-term wealth when it seemed that everyone around him was getting rich overnight was a critical part of his business genius.

By 1870, Rockefeller and Flagler knew that the oil industry was in trouble. For ten years it had offered huge profits with little cost and even less skill. All a farm boy had to do was lay claim to a tract of land, build a derrick, and drill a hole. If he struck oil, he was rich—at least in the beginning. As the decade progressed, and the Civil War ended and lowered demand, the amount of oil produced began to exceed the market capacity. This oversupply caused oil prices to fluctuate wildly, but the

Henry Morrison Flagler believed that ". . . friendship founded on business is better than business founded on friendship."

long-term trend was downward. By 1870, the country was awash in oil. Overproduction had driven the price so low that few were making a profit.

This surplus did not only affect the crude oil producers. By 1870, refining capacity was three times higher than demand. In addition, the oil industry itself was grossly inefficient. During the years of easy profits, most refiners had been concerned only with producing the greatest amount of kerosene as quickly as possible. With the profit margins high, it took a refiner with a long range vision to concentrate on efficiency.

Rockefeller did concern himself with efficiency and even in the glutted market of 1870 he was able to make a profit. But it was obvious that continued surplus would drive the price of kerosene so low that even he would not be able to stay in business.

Rockefeller and Flagler realized that they could no longer focus only on their company. Their continued success was dependent on the well-being of the industry as a whole. They became convinced that there should be a guiding organization, or a *cartel*, that could create more cooperation and less competition.

It may come as a surprise to discover that a titan of American business felt that the free market needed to be controlled. Today, we tend to think of all business leaders as believers in the idea that the free market will fix most problems. Rockefeller and several of the other giants of nineteenth-century capitalism, however, came to hold the view that unfettered capitalism was inefficient and ultimately destructive. The great banker of the era, J. P. Morgan, spent most of his career forcing competing railroad barons to cooperate. His influence on credit markets allowed him to keep money from flowing to railroad construction that he thought unnecessary. Why build two roads going to the same place when one was adequate? Morgan used his power to smooth out what he saw as the illogical motivations of the railroad barons. This view was contrary to the ideas of classical economists, such as Adam Smith, who had said that when overproduction made a business unprofitable, the activity in that business would decline. Those businesses that remained would then begin to make a profit. In other words, only the most efficient and profitable organizations would survive.

Rockefeller was not an economist, however. He was a businessman who did not like what he saw. The oil industry did not seem to be following the pattern predicted by the classical economists. Although the price of oil had dropped to a fraction of what it had been in 1860, new wells were being drilled every day, and refineries were still being built.

Rockefeller decided to do two things. First, he knew that many refiners were not profitable. Now was a good time to buy them up. Second, there needed to be agreements between the large refiners, large producers, and the railroads that would allow the giants in the industry to be assured of a profit. It was much more expensive in the late-nineteenth century than it is today to get goods to market. Shipping costs ate up a much higher percentage of a producer's profits. Essentially, Rockefeller wanted to create a cartel to insulate the interests of a few from the market fluctuations caused by many.

To carry out his plan, Rockefeller needed more capital. The partnership of Rockefeller, Andrews and Flagler had used both funds generated by their business and monies borrowed from banks to finance expansion. Now they needed a new way to raise vast amounts of capital.

Rockefeller and Flagler's solution to this problem was to form a joint stock company. On January 10, 1870, the firm of Rockefeller, Andrews and Flagler was replaced by the new corporation, Standard Oil of Ohio. Worth $1 million, it was the largest capitalized company in the United States. At its inception, Standard Oil of Ohio controlled ten percent of the oil refining business. It owned a barrel-making plant, tank cars, and shipping facilities, in addition to its refineries. The new firm found simple offices in downtown Cleveland that did little to suggest its size and power.

Rockefeller owned more shares of the company than anyone else. Over the years he took every opportunity to buy any available shares. His confidence in his ability to manage a company to dominance, even in an industry as troubled as oil, never wavered.

The incorporation of Standard Oil helped to raise

money. The success of the stock sale was limited, however, by the refusal of most large investors to take an interest. Rockefeller still needed more assistance if he was going to be able to carry out his plan to consolidate the industry. What he did next would insure his reputation as the "dark man" of American industry. Up until 1872, Rockefeller was increasingly feared in the oil fields of Pennsylvania. After 1872, Rockefeller was the most well-known—and most hated—name in the business.

As he sought a way to bring order to the oil business, Rockefeller was approached by the management of three of the largest railroads. The railroads had been locked in fierce competition, cutting rates so deeply to attract business that they were no longer profitable. The railroads were buckling beneath the weight of the competition and had hit upon a plan to solve their problems. In order for it to work, they needed the cooperation of Standard Oil, the largest of the oil companies.

The railroads, which had a dominant influence in Pennsylvania politics, had attained a charter from the state legislature for an organization they named the South Improvement Company (SIC). When Rockefeller and Flagler met with Tom Scott, the president of the Pennsylvania Railroad, in late 1871, Scott had a proposal that excited the usually unflappable Rockefeller.

The South Improvement scheme was simple and ruthless. The railroads would raise freight rates for all refiners. However, the refiners in the scheme, primarily Standard Oil, would receive a fifty percent rebate on the freight they shipped. This rebate was not available to refiners outside the scheme.

This part of the SIC plan was audacious enough, but there was more. In addition to the rebates received for barrels of oil shipped, Standard Oil would be paid another rebate, called a *drawback*, for shipments made by *other* refiners! In return for the rebates, the railroads wanted Standard Oil to agree to ship all of its freight on three roads: the Pennsylvania, the New York Central, and the Erie.

Naturally, the members of the South Improvement plan were sworn to secrecy. Rockefeller thought that the plan was the best for everyone. He even said that the farm boys who were trying to strike it rich in oil would be happier back following a mule in the fields. He rationalized that he was doing the weaker producers and refiners a favor by pushing them out of the business.

The SIC leaders' oath of secrecy was of little use. Within a month of the agreement, in February 1872, word began to spread throughout the oil region that freight rates would soon be doubled on everyone but a few large refiners. The region erupted into anger and near violence almost overnight. Inevitably, the details of the so-called secret agreement were leaked and the leaders of the South Improvement Company were labeled as "thieves" and "monsters."

Although he was only one of the conspirators and not

the one who first proposed the idea, Rockefeller soon emerged as the most notorious. Newspapers in the oil patch framed his portrait in black and denounced him as an evil genius bent on destroying their lives and work.

Organized resistance to the plan was quick to materialize. The oil producers created their own organization and agreed to boycott Standard Oil and any company participating in the plan. At first, Rockefeller and the other leaders of the SIC did not think the boycott would work. But, to their surprise, Standard Oil soon had to lay off most of its work force.

Rockefeller was determined to ride out the trouble. Standard Oil had the resources to withstand a long fight. But the railroads had more debt and began to crumble under the pressure. Even the Pennsylvania legislature, which was usually firmly in the grasp of the railroads, began to feel the pressure of its constituents who were angry over the collusion of capital and politics.

By the end of March 1872, the South Improvement Company was officially terminated. The three railroads agreed to rescind the agreement and to apply uniform rates across the board. The small producers and refiners had won—for now.

The seeds of most of Rockefeller's future legal and political troubles were germinated in the SIC affair. One observer of bad sentiment toward Rockefeller was a school girl named Ida Tarbell, whose father owned a small well near Oil Creek. Years later, in a journalistic attack on Standard Oil, she wrote:

> I remember a night when my father came home
> with a grim look on his face and told how he with
> scores of other producers had signed a pledge not
> to sell to the Cleveland ogre that also had profited
> from the scheme . . . a new name, that of Standard
> Oil Company, replac[ed] the name South Im-
> provement Company in popular contempt.

In the ensuing years, Rockefeller often grumbled that he did not understand what all the fuss was about. "There never was a shipment made or a rebate or drawback collected under the South Improvement plan," he said. He always claimed that the plan had been a sincere effort to steady prices and to bring order to the industry, and he insisted that he had only gone along with the plan to prove to the railroads that it would not work.

It seemed in the spring of 1872 that Rockefeller had been vanquished. It soon came clear, however, that the collapse of the SIC was only a temporary victory for his rivals. The market forces that had created the SIC were still in place. Rockefeller could no more be stopped from taking advantage of every opportunity to build up his business then the producers could be made to stop drilling wells.

Rockefeller and Flagler continued to work to consoli-date the industry. Although the SIC had failed, the publicity worked in Standard Oil's favor, as many refiners decided to sell before they went backrupt. Rockefeller spent much of his time during the winter of 1872 buying up the competition in Cleveland. Their first approach to competitors was "soft." First, they politely made a business offer to the owner, willingly showing him evidence of Standard's profits and low-cost structure to convince him that his company could not compete with Standard. They hoped the refiner would see that it was in his best interest to join them. If this overture was rejected, they began lowering their prices in the other company's territory until the rival suffered such a loss that its owner really had no choice but to sell to Rockefeller.

Using the leverage of the short-lived SIC, Standard had bought up the vast majority of rival Cleveland refiners by the end of 1872. This rapid consolidation became known as the "Cleveland Massacre." As successful as it was as a business move, it did even more damage to Rockefeller's reputation. When accused of intimidating his competition to sell, he lashed out at what he called "an absolute lie." He said most of the refiners knew they were already doomed by the "ruinous competition." The chance to sell out to Standard and receive Standard shares "was a godsend to them all."

The heavy reliance on secrecy, insisted on by Rockefeller, also hurt his reputation. Part of Standard tactics was to use code names. For example, Baltimore was "Droplet," Philadelphia was "Drugget," refiners were "Douters," and "Amelia" meant that everything was fine. One of Rockefeller's favorite expressions was: "Success comes froms keeping the ears open and the mouth closed."

Certainly, Standard was emerging as the winner of the "oil war." It controlled ninety percent of refining by 1879, as well as the pipelines of western Pennsylvania. Furthermore, the railroads were so dependent on Standard's business that he was able to dictate his own freight terms.

One project did defy Rockefeller's control: the Tidewater Pipeline. This incredible pipeline extended for 110 miles to various railroad connections and has been compared to the Brooklyn Bridge as a technological feat of the time. As it came under intense pressure from Standard, its builders used secrecy as effectively as Rockefeller and Flagler. They even released fake route surveys until it was completed. For the first time, the railroads felt the punch of competition. Rockefeller responded by building four longer pipelines to Cleveland, Buffalo, New York, and Philadelphia. He also managed to buy shares in the Tidewater Company, although not enough to control it.

Chapter Five

The Trust

John D. Rockefeller believed that his talent at making money was a God-given gift; one that he had to develop: "I believe it is my duty to make money and still more money, and to use the money I make for the good of my fellow man according to the dictates of my conscience." As a follower of the Baptist moral code for an orderly life, Rockefeller saw it as his responsibility to bring order to the oil business. A devout churchgoer and Sunday-school teacher, he used the language and imagery of the Bible. *Salvation, miracles, Noah's ark, the angel of mercy, Moses, missionary service, serving the devil,* and *the Slough of Despond* were just a few of the religious phrases and ideas that peppered his conversations.

This merging of religious fervor with business shrewdness provided him an unmatched single-mindedness that steadied him as he built his enterprise. But it also blinded him to his own shortcomings. He was able, without a hint of irony, to excuse his own actions while he quickly condemned the same in others.

"Self-righteous" and "icy" were adjectives frequently used to describe him, but his family knew a different man. He and Cettie had six children. He grieved deeply when they lost a one-year-old baby. He could be found evenings and weekends playing silly games with his five remaining children—four daughters and one son, the baby, called Junior. One game, called Buzz, consisted of the players taking turns while counting quickly. When the number seven came up, the counter was out if he did not say "Buzz!" instead of seven. Another of his favorite tricks was to balance a plate on his nose or to catch a cracker in his mouth when it fell from his nose. He loved to get the children laughing uproariously.

He loved riding horses and carriage driving. This relaxed him, as did naps on his couch in the office and working out with the simple exercise equipment of the day. He taught his children to swim, row, bicycle, ride horseback, and to ice skate. He was particularly fond of ice skating and enjoyed it into old age. He began playing golf at middle age, and it soon became a passion that determined the routine of his daily life after he retired.

As he grew wealthier, Rockefeller began buying and building nice homes. He kept his Cleveland residence at 424 Euclid Avenue and bought a summer estate not far away that his family enjoyed called Forest Hill. After Standard Oil left Cleveland and moved its headquarters to New York City in 1883, Rockefeller bought a home at Four West Fifty-fourth Street, where the Museum of

The Rockefeller children in 1885: (From left to right) Alta, Bessie, Edith, and Junior.
(Courtesy of the Rockefeller Archive Center.)

Modern Art now stands. Later estates were developed at Pocantico Hills north of New York City on the Hudson River, and at Lakewood, New Jersey. When he was old, he added a relatively more modest home called The Casements at Ormond Beach, Florida, where he spent his winters playing golf.

The Rockefellers lived a simple, thrifty lifestyle within the fine houses. They did not dress lavishly and their children wore hand-me-downs. There was one tricycle the children had to share. Junior had to walk to school and earn his spending money by working on the estates for the same wages as the laborers. Church and Sunday school were a part of every week, and prayers a part of every day.

Rockefeller's relationship with his employees was courteous and cordial. Those who worked around him, in Cleveland or New York, knew he kept a very regular schedule. He moved about quietly and calmly and had an unsettling knack for entering the office without anyone noticing he was there. Everyone agreed that he was even-tempered; he did not shout or rage, but kept his emotions under control. This was a valuable gift and contributed to his success, but his emotional control also added to his reputation for secretive ruthlessness.

After moving to New York, Rockefeller met daily at noon with his small group of executives at 26 Broadway for a business lunch. He did not sit at the head of the table and liked to get every man's opinion before giving his own. He operated by consensus. He wanted all decisions to be unanimously accepted by this close-knit and tight-lipped group of men that included Henry Flagler, William Rockefeller, John Archbold, Charles Pratt, and Henry H. Rogers.

Rockefeller paid his salaried and hourly employees above-average wages and provided for their pensions. As did most businessmen of his era, he loathed the idea of unions and did not recognize the legitimacy of organized labor. Paying higher than average salaries was one way to keep unions out of Standard Oil. He encouraged non-drinking and churchgoing among all his employees.

Rockefeller may have been convinced that God gave him his money, but it soon became obvious that many thought he had made a pact with the devil. His long legal battle with his enemies began in April 1879, when a grand jury in Clarion County, Pennsylvania, indicted him, Flagler, and other Standard officials for conspiracy to monopolize oil and to extort railroad rebates. While no one was overly concerned that the lawsuits would result in any severe penalties for the men or for Standard Oil, the legal process could have forced them to open their internal books and operations to the public. They spent a great deal of time and effort avoiding this. Rockefeller himself stayed out of Pennsylvania and tried to extract a promise that he would not be extradited (officially handed over by the legal system) from New York to Pennsylvania. For the next thirty years, he tried to stay out of court and ahead of the law. As more laws were passed, such as the Interstate Commerce Act of 1887 and the Sherman Antitrust Act of 1890, this became increasingly difficult.

As the company came under attack, Rockefeller and the other officers knew they needed to find a way to protect it. It had grown into a huge organization with various units. Oil was only one of the ways the company made money; by 1882 the transportation business was a larger part of the company than the refineries.

They needed some way to manage this unwieldy beast, but were hampered by antiquated laws that did not allow for interstate corporations. One company could not hold stock in another, unless the state legislature gave it special permission. This procedure of legislatures granting ownership rights was the source of a great deal of corruption.

A corporation was limited to exist inside the single state that issued its charter. This meant that Standard Oil Corporation could not own refineries outside of Ohio. This presented a dilemma to Standard Oil of Ohio. They were rapidly acquiring refineries, pipelines, and other facilities in various states. They needed a way to protect their interests, especially with the mounting legal challenges they faced.

Rockefeller and his lawyers hit on a device that gave them a way around the legal restrictions. While the law prohibited a corporation to own other corporations, it did not prohibit *stockholders,* such as those who owned Standard Oil of Ohio, from legally owning another cor-

John Archbold was an outspoken executive of Standard Oil.

poration. In short, they decided to make a distinction between personal and corporate property.

The first step was to set up a Standard Oil in each state: Standard Oil of New York, Standard Oil of New Jersey, etc. Then the stock of each of these new corporations was held in "trust" by a board of trustees that was given the responsibility to undertake the "general supervision" of each of the companies. This Board of Trustees then appointed managers to run each part of the vast organization in tandem with the other parts.

Committees were created for the following divisions: domestic trade, export trade, manufacturing, staves and heading, pipeline, case, lubricating, and production. The managers of each division sent daily reports to the Executive Committee of about fifteen men who met at 26 Broadway in New York City and analyzed, discussed, and made recommendations to the committees. This model provided consistent top-down policy based on local control of production details. In 1883, when the trust was formed, John D. Rockefeller owned more than a third of the trust certificates, worth about $20 million.

With the creation of the trust, Standard Oil became virtually the only kerosene and lubricant company that most Americans knew existed. They were highly successful at providing low-cost products, including kerosene for lamps, lubricants for moving parts of machines, gasoline for solvents, gas for illuminating entire buildings, petroleum jelly for skin moisturizing and healing, and paraffin for food preservation and chewing gum.

Rockefeller was clearly a new type of businessman. He had the classic entrepreneurial courage and skill at seizing an opportunity. But unlike most entrepreneurs, who often lose interest in their businesses once they get going, Rockefeller was also a highly skillful manager who was able to direct his company into a mature organization.

Still in his early forties in the early 1880s, when Standard Oil products had eighty-five percent of the market, Rockefeller focused on operating his company on some basic principles. He scrupulously calculated costs, sometimes to three decimal places. Communications were recorded and responded to by the appropriate individual or committee. Addresses of every oil buyer in the country were maintained, as was a sales summary of what the independent dealers were doing. All top managers were strong, assertive men (including Rockefeller's brother William and Henry Flagler), so Rockefeller insisted executive decisions be made by consensus to minimize personality clashes. He always maintained good credit with bankers, repaying loans on time and keeping a cash reserve, even if it meant lowering share dividends. Finally, because he believed that oil was a permanently valuable resource, he never passed up a chance to buy when prices fell. He said that it was important to not lose one's nerve when the market was depressed. He clearly followed this last principle when, in the mid-1880s, oil was discovered in Ohio and Indiana.

He started buying up all the oil he could, storing it in huge tanks. Over the years, as oil exploration moved farther west and south, and later to vast reaches of the globe, Standard continued to move in and buy up resources. Rockefeller judged that control of eighty-five percent of the market was enough to give Standard Oil the ideal stability.

This business philosophy resulted in Standard Oil attaining what economists would later call "vertical integration." This meant they controlled all aspects of procurement, production, and distribution. Rockefeller was able to translate his personal drive for stability into an organization that guaranteed an orderly flow from natural resource, to product, to consumer.

Rockefeller met some internal resistance in his drive to vertically integrate Standard Oil. He often had to convince his Executive Committee to make investments and to purchase vast amounts of oil to be stored. Some directors argued that buying oil to store was an inefficient way to use their capital. But he firmly believed in the future of the business, and even the most wary executive eventually gave way to his determination.

During the years of consolidation, Standard Oil gave money to politicians and legislators. Some called this practice bribery, others extortion. Rockefeller agreed with other businessmen of the era who thought there was nothing wrong with contributing money to politicians who shared his ideas. Critics disagreed and called it collusion. As the nineteenth century was drawing to a close, the most divisive issue in American politics was the clashing attitudes between the businessmen such as Rockefeller and the growing group of intellectuals, ministers, politicians, and social workers of the so-called progressive movement who wanted to hem in the power of the corporation.

Chapter Six

The Philanthropist Emerges

If John D. Rockefeller believed that God had given him his money, as he said many times, he also believed that God expected him to use his wealth for the betterment of humankind. From the beginning of his life Rockefeller gave away money. As a boy under the direction of his mother, he took coins from his blue bowl "bank" on the fireplace mantel to give to the Baptist congregation. His personal account books show that as a young man in Cleveland, he donated to a Methodist church, a German Sunday school, an African-American church, and Catholic orphans.

His first contributions after he became a wealthy businessman were often to universities. He gave to Denison University, a Baptist college in Ohio. He was also very generous to A.C. Bacone's Indian University in the Oklahoma Territory. He gave to Barnard College and Cornell University, both located in New York.

In June 1882, two women who had once been affiliated with Cettie's former college, spoke to a group of Cleveland Baptists about their work at the Atlanta Baptist Female Seminary for young African-American women in Georgia. Cettie and Rockefeller listened as Sophia Packard and Harriet Giles described the cramped, damp basement of the Friendship Baptist Church, vividly depicting the appalling conditions that both the students and teachers endured at the makeshift school. Rockefeller was moved by their talk, and after he was assured that Packard and Giles had made a long-term commitment to their endeavor, he donated enough money to found the college on a secure base. Packard and Giles offered to name the school after him, but he asked instead that it be named for his in-laws, who had been ardent, active abolitionists and supporters of education. Spelman Seminary aimed to give Christian training to its students. In the style of Booker T. Washington's Tuskeegee Institute, it also gave young women job and craft skills. The school became Spelman College in 1924 and eventually acquired a national reputation. The mother and grandmother of Martin Luther King, Jr. were alumnae.

Rockefeller wanted his donation to Spelman College to provide an incentive for others to give. This method of donating money evolved into the "matching grant" that is so common today. Rockefeller also provided expert advice to Henry Morehouse, the secretary of the American Baptist Home Mission Society, and to others who were working to help the poor.

In the early 1880s, a Baptist minister from Cleveland

began to badger Rockefeller to found a great Baptist university. The Reverend Charles Strong was worried that the brightest young Baptists were going to schools like Harvard, Yale, and Princeton and falling under the influence of "modernism" or of other faiths. He wanted to found a "university of the future" in New York City for graduate students and researchers only. With his experience as president of Rochester Theological Seminary, Strong felt he was the perfect man to run the new school.

Rockefeller liked Strong personally, and Strong's brilliant philosopher son Charles would soon win the heart of Bessie, Rockefeller's oldest child. The young couple was married in 1889, at the end of Bessie's junior year at Vassar, and their families were thus united. Meanwhile, Reverend Strong, who was often bossy and presumptuous, relentlessly advocated the school to Rockefeller. His oppressive nature soon convinced Rockefeller that giving money away was often as stressful as making it in the first place.

Thomas Goodspeed of the Baptist Union Theological Seminary near Chicago introduced Rockefeller to the young, charismatic, and academically brilliant William Rainey Harper. Harper had left the Baptist Union Theological Seminary to teach at Yale. Goodspeed suggested to Rockefeller that the Midwest needed a university that would both keep brilliant faculty, such as Harper, and attract top quality students.

Harper had earned his Ph.D. at eighteen, opened five Bible schools and a correspondence school, and had started an American Institute of Hebrew. He was among the most distinguished American Biblical scholars. Rockefeller's daughter Bessie was a student at Vassar College where Harper lectured on Sundays. When Rockefeller visited Bessie, he got to know the young teacher better.

Rockefeller began to seriously consider building a Baptist-affiliated university in the Midwest. He was further convinced in 1888 when he read a report by another brilliant Baptist minister, Frederick T. Gates. Gates's report, entitled "The Need for a Baptist University in Chicago," presented concrete facts, figures, and proposals that appealed to Rockefeller. Gates became his top advisor on the project. On May 18, 1889, Gates announced to the American Baptist Education Society that Rockefeller had pledged $600,000 to build a school in Chicago. Great cheers and singing erupted. Rockefeller gave the Baptists one year to come up with an additional $400,000 to prove that the institution could become independent of him.

Again, Rockefeller refused use of his name for the new school. Though he admired Andrew Carnegie's gift of 2800 free libraries in the United States, he shied from the fact that the giver's name was chiseled in stone on each building. He would not even allow an oil lamp to appear in the school emblem for fear that someone would believe it to be a lamp lit by Standard Oil.

Rockefeller saw colleges and universities as institutions that spread culture and fought ignorance. His guiding principle for recipients of his money was to root out the causes that created beggars so that the institutions could find solutions to poverty.

William Rainey Harper was Rockefeller's choice for president of the new University of Chicago. Rockefeller told him to get the very best professors, and Harper did just that, although this multiplied the cost. The construction costs also multiplied. Soon expenses mounted far beyond what Rockefeller had intended, but he continued to donate money.

The tensions over building the University of Chicago came at a time when Rockefeller was not feeling well physically or psychologically. He had been under twenty years of never-ending strain while building Standard Oil and was constantly receiving requests for charity. In 1888, Cettie was badly burned when an alcohol lamp exploded. Her health slowly deteriorated in other ways, too. In 1891, Rockefeller caught a bad flu that was sweeping the country and was unable to work for weeks. He began to notice other ailments. Today his condition would be contributed to overwork and stress.

His doctor ordered him to work less and sent him to Forest Hill for isolation from his business world. John Archbold had by then replaced Henry Flagler as his top executive, and he filled in now for Rockefeller. Frederick Gates became Rockefeller's "gatekeeper" for philan-

John D. Rockefeller provided the money to found the University of Chicago.

thropy, filtering requests for financial assistance. After eight months of working his Forest Hill farm and basking in the pastoral life, Rockefeller felt restored. He also realized that he did not want to return to the business world and should gradually retire.

Harper had promised that the University of Chicago would open in 1892. It did, but it was much transformed from the little college Rockefeller had envisioned. Harper had managed, with Rockefeller's money, to build a new school that almost instantly ranked with the best eastern universities in terms of enrollment and the quality of its teachers. Besides its famous professors, it began with 750 students, including twenty-five percent women and a few

Catholics, Jews, and African Americans. The campus had been built on land donated by Marshall Field, next to the Midway of the world-famous Columbian Exposition of 1893.

Harper could not stop himself from overspending. He would not agree with Rockefeller that a university had to balance its books. The two men fell into a pattern. After protesting, Rockefeller would give more money. Then the same thing would happen again. Gates scolded and warned, too. Finally, Rockefeller cut off money and banned Harper from ever talking about money to him again. Gates and Junior were appointed to the university board to try to keep a handle on financial matters.

Although Rockefeller paid for most of the founding of the University of Chicago, he did not interfere with what was taught. Even his brother William thought the university was a mistake: "You are getting together a lot of scribblers, a crowd of Socialists who won't do any good," he warned. Indeed, one of the most famous and influential critics of "the captains of industry" was the University of Chicago sociologist Thorstein Veblen, who published *The Theory of the Leisure Class* in 1899. Veblen created the term "conspicuous consumption" for the tasteless flaunting of wealth by the newly rich—something that Rockefeller and Cettie were certainly not guilty of.

His conflicts with Harper did not turn Rockefeller away from funding other schools. In 1901, he founded the Rockefeller Institute for Medical Research (RIMR) in

New York City. (In the 1950s, the name changed to Rockefeller University, and it continues to flourish today.) Although he allowed the use of his name this time, he learned from his University of Chicago experience with William Rainey Harper not to give too much money at the outset. He was determined to force the school's directors to collect money from other benefactors. He and Gates also kept future plans from administrators so they would not be tempted to spend more.

Simon Flexner, the scientist who headed RIMR, was quite different from Harper in style and approach. He worked to bring in scientists who wanted to study and make experiments in an effort to find cures for diseases. He also saw the value of "pure" or "basic" research and allowed scientists to work on research that had no direct connection to a specific disease. As he put it, "There is no useless knowledge in medical research. Ideas may come to us out of order in point of time."

Chapter Seven

Whipping Time

After the failure of the South Improvement scheme in 1872, Standard Oil developed less obvious means to gain advantage over its competitors. To Rockefeller, the less competition the better. He saw no reason for there to be other oil companies and wrote in letters that Standard should take all the business there was.

Standard Oil used several measures to control the market. Whenever possible, they simply undersold the competition in an area until they drove them out of business. In other instances, they warned stores and dry goods shops that sold kerosene that they would lose their Standard supply if they insisted on selling a competitor's product as well. They also threatened to fund other stores that would drive down prices if the retailer continued to sell the competitor's kerosene. Another favorite trick was to buy up all the barrels in a refiner's area—thus denying him a way to ship his product. Standard had begun making its own barrels years before when Rockefeller noticed that the man Standard bought barrels from, a Mr.

Hopper, had built a big house on top of a hill outside of Cleveland. "Whew! It's an expensive house, isn't it?" Rockefeller said as he passed by it on a train. "I wonder if Mr. Hopper isn't making altogether too much money? Let's look into it." After checking the books, he decided that Mr. Hopper was indeed making too much money and canceled the contract with his company.

Rockefeller was ruthless when it came to controlling cost and driving out competition. Although he invested in building a barrel plant, he did not hesitate to invest even more money in tank cars, which did not use barrels, when he became convinced it would save on shipping costs. Once, while walking through the refinery, he watched as a worker soldered a lid onto a barrel. "How many drops of solder do you use in each can?" he asked. When the worker replied that he used forty drops, he asked: "Have you tried thirty-eight?" When it turned out that the can could be sealed with only thirty-nine drops, he ordered the decrease. He later bragged that this change saved $2500 the first year.

By 1890, John D. Rockefeller was the wealthiest man in the world, and Standard Oil dominated the oil industry. But he was soon to discover that his wealth and power could not protect him from public opinion. The coming criticism from politicians and journalists underscored that one of his greatest strengths in business—his ability to keep his plans secret—was a weakness when he was attacked in newspapers and in legislatures. As the greater public was presented with the picture of Standard Oil as a monster operated by an evil genius, Rockefeller kept silent, allowing the charges to gain credibility.

Despite Rockefeller's deeply held belief that he had helped the oil business—and the industrial development of the United States—by working to end unbridled competition with its ruinous cycle of boom-and-bust, most people were angered when news of rebates and other special deals with the railroads became public knowledge. Newspaper cartoonists were soon representing Standard Oil as an octopus or an anaconda, operated by arrogant, secretive, ruthless men. Some journalists made their reputations by attacking Rockefeller and his company.

William Demarest Lloyd became one of the first to earn a national reputation as an enemy of Standard Oil. He began writing about the company during the 1880s in articles read by the well-informed subscribers to the *Atlantic Monthly* magazine. Because he was a wealthy man himself, Lloyd had access to many influential people, especially in his hometown of Chicago.

Lloyd heard Rockefeller testify in 1887 before the new Interstate Commerce Commission and was overwhelmed with disgust for him. He saw Rockefeller as the embodiment of evil, and he set out to destroy him in a book. In *Wealth Against Commonwealth*, published in 1894 but excerpted earlier for magazines, Lloyd argued that Rockefeller and the other directors of the oil trust were

William Demarest Lloyd wrote articles denouncing Standard Oil in the *Atlantic Monthly*.

little more than common criminals who "ought to be in the penitentiary." He accused Rockefeller of creating phony shortages in order to run up prices, and he claimed that the South Improvement Company had not been disbanded, but only driven underground, where it continued to do its evil work.

Lloyd's book had some trouble finding a publisher, but when it was finally released it became a sensation. One critic called it the most important book since *Uncle Tom's Cabin*, which had appeared fifty years before. Although there were many errors of fact in his work, and Standard Oil did have some defenders, Rockefeller's refusal to respond gave the greatest impression. Rockefeller apparently thought that by not responding he would indicate that the charges were beneath contempt. Instead, his silence convinced many that the book had the basis of truth.

Although Lloyd's attack created a sensation among the readers of the somewhat elitist *Atlantic Monthly*, it was not until an even more effective author published another attack on Standard Oil in a more widely circulated magazine that Rockefeller-hating became a wildly popular American sport.

Between 1902 and 1904, the journalist Ida Tarbell presented in *McClure's Magazine* her perspective on Standard Oil and its war against independent refiners, transporters, and producers. Tarbell wrote very clearly and forcefully. She was in her mid-forties when she began working on this—her most famous piece.

This was the book Ida Tarbell had been wanting to write for years. She was from the Pennsylvania oil country. Her father had begun making tank containers right after Drake discovered oil, and he had allied with the oil producers against the South Improvement Company in 1872. Her brother was an officer of the Pure Oil Company, one of the few competitors who survived Standard Oil. She personally blamed Rockefeller for the failure of her father's business and did not accept Rockefeller's idea that consolidation, at least not the way he effected it through Standard Oil, was good for the industry. She saw it as conspiracy against small businesspeople such as her father.

Tarbell had her own memories of Titusville, and her brother at the Pure Oil Company was more than willing to feed her information on Standard Oil. She still wanted to get an inside look at how the company worked, but this seemed virtually impossible because of Rockefeller's policy of total secrecy.

Then Tarbell got a break through her friend Mark Twain. Earlier, when Twain had faced bankruptcy, he had been saved by top Standard executive, Henry H. Rogers, who loved Twain's works. Rogers straightened out the author's accounting and then continued to control and invest his money with great success. Twain, who called Rogers his best friend, told the Standard executive about the intelligent blind and deaf girl Helen Keller, and Rogers paid for her education at Radcliffe College.

Twain was connected with *McClure's Magazine*, and when Rogers heard about the series of articles that were to be published there, he asked Twain to find out more about Tarbell and her proposed series. Twain arranged for an interview between the two. Rogers and Tarbell liked each other and found that they had not lived far apart as children in the same Pennsylvania oil country. As Rogers understood it, Tarbell's articles were to be "a narrative history of Standard Oil." Tarbell said they were not intended to be controversial, but rather a straightforward narrative. Rogers agreed to be interviewed.

As the articles were published, it became clear that Rogers had made a mistake. Standard Oil was represented as a giant villain working to destroy the virtuous, struggling independents. The series became a sensation, and because no one at Standard fought back or presented contrary evidence to Tarbell's charges, other people came forward with their grievances. Soon, Rockefeller was the most hated man in America, and Standard Oil was the most hated company in the world.

Tarbell's series ran for two years in twenty-four installments. The articles were published in a book, *The History of Standard Oil,* in 1904. In 1905, Tarbell published a personal portrait of John D. Rockefeller in *McClure's*. She judged him to be a Christian hypocrite who "systematically played with loaded dice" in his business dealings and never competed fairly. In this portrait, for which she had no personal interview with

Journalist Ida Tarbell, who grew up in the Pennsylvania oil country, wrote a series of articles attacking the practices of John D. Rockefeller and Standard Oil.

Rockefeller, she also found him to be physically, as well as morally, repulsive. In the fall of 1903, she sneaked into his Sunday school class at the Euclid Avenue Baptist Church in Cleveland to get a look at him and listen to him. She then called him "a living mummy" and his church activity a "hypocritical facade brilliantly created by the predatory businessman."

Tarbell had her researcher dig up all he could about Rockefeller's father, Big Bill. They tried to track him down but did not succeed. "Doc" Rockefeller's double life was not revealed until two years after his death in 1906, when a reporter for Joseph Pulitzer's *New York World* presented his story in 1908 as a headline-grabbing exposé.

Although Ida Tarbell did Rockefeller immense harm, he took it stoically and in keeping with his policy of public silence. The only anger he showed was to sometimes refer to her when he was with friends as "Miss Tar Barrel."

The publication of the attacks by Lloyd and Tarbell set off an avalanche of what we today call bad press. From this time on, he would symbolize everything that was wrong with American capitalism. But Rockefeller showed that he, and Standard Oil, could withstand the pressure from a journalist. The next set of attacks on his life's work, however, was to come from a much more powerful source, and would forever alter the structure and mission of the company he founded.

Chapter Eight

Break Up

Ironically, the next stage of attacks on Standard Oil came after Rockefeller had retired from day-to-day operations. A combination of his health worries and the time he had to spend in his philanthropic work eventually persuaded him to retire. Although the exact date of his retirement is unknown, he had essentially stopped working by 1897.

Rockefeller often said that the real pleasure of his life was his family. He and Cettie had five children, four of whom lived to adulthood. After their oldest daughter, Bessie, married Charles Strong, she left Vassar and went to Germany with her husband. Charles and Bessie lived in Chicago and New York while he taught philosophy and wrote books. In 1902, Bessie had a stroke and began spending most of her time in bed. She died in 1906.

Alta Rockefeller was born in 1871, after Alice, who died as an infant. Alta loved her family and always tried to do what she thought would please her parents. Alta became a social worker. In Manhattan she set up a school to teach poor girls to sew for a living. She started a clinic there, too, for chronically sick women. In Cleveland she founded the Alta House, a day care and kindergarten for the children of poor Italian immigrants. She worked at these places herself. In 1901, she married Parmalee Prentice, a brilliant lawyer who had degrees from Amherst College and Harvard Law School. Alta and Prentice had three children. Alta outlived her siblings, dying in 1962.

The most flamboyant of the Rockefeller children was Edith, the fourth child. She was certainly unlike her parents. As a child, Edith was the most willful, outspoken, and the most intellectual. She married Harold McCormick (the grandson of Cyrus McCormick, who had invented the mechanical reaper) in 1895 and moved to Chicago. Shaken by the death of two of her children, Edith and Harold sought therapy at the famous Swiss clinic of Dr. Carl Jung. She found time to act as a patron for artists and writers she met in Europe. One writer she befriended and supported was the Irish novelist James Joyce, to whom she sent regular checks during the eight years he was writing his masterpiece, *Ulysses*. Eventually, Edith and Harold both became involved in affairs and divorced. She died of cancer in 1932.

John D. Rockefeller, Jr., was the fifth child and the only son of John and Cettie. Junior was raised at home with his sisters. He had few boys of his own social class to play with. With his sisters he had to earn his own money by performing household chores (for example, one penny for every ten weeds pulled in the yard, fifteen cents for chopping a cord of wood) and show his account ledger to his mother or father.

When he began school in New York City at age twelve, he had to walk to class, although other boys were driven. He was a very good student who earned high grades and learned to play the violin well. He worked so hard to get a ninety-eight percent average in 1887 that he had a nervous collapse. Rockefeller sent him to Forest Hill for the rest of the school year to do hard outdoor work. Cettie went too, but whereas Junior was rejuvenated, she became weaker and even more of a shut-in.

Junior finished high school in the Browning School, a special school his father and Uncle William set up for him, his cousins, and a few other wealthy boys whose like-minded parents did not want them slipping into loose ways and undisciplined study.

Junior attended Brown University in Providence, Rhode Island. It was a wonderful and liberating experience for him. In an ethics class at this Baptist college, for example, he heard more than he ever had about the moral responsibility of the businessman for the welfare of his employees. While at Brown, Junior met and fell in love with Abby Aldrich, the daughter of the powerful senator from Rhode Island, Nelson Aldrich. The couple was married in 1901.

After Junior graduated from Brown (with an average high enough to get him into the Phi Beta Kappa Honor

Society), he knew he would work for his father, but Rockefeller had not made it clear what he was to do. Junior began by ordering and shipping items for the Rockefeller homes. Frederick Gates then became a mentor, acquainting him with the philanthropies and industries. Before he was thirty, Junior was on the boards of the University of Chicago, U.S. Steel, and Standard Oil.

As Rockefeller quietly slipped into retirement and focused more on his family and golf, he came under increasing attack by journalists and politicians. As early as 1890, the attorney general of Standard's home state of Ohio had sued the company in state court. The attorney general argued that the trust arrangement that held Standard Oil together as a legal entity had been violated by the way the boards of the various companies were interlocked. In 1892, the Supreme Court of Ohio ruled that Standard Oil of Ohio would have to pull out of the trust.

Undeterred, Rockefeller gathered the board and lawyers together in New York and worked out a new scheme that circumvented the court's decision and left control of the various companies in the same hands as before.

Although Rockefeller had found a way around the decision of the Ohio court, a challenge from a much more formidable opponent was on the horizon.

Theodore Roosevelt was a member of the Republican Party, as was Rockefeller and most of the other directors of the trust. For years, the Republicans had protected the trusts. That made the attacks that came down on Standard

John D. Rockefeller, Jr., would succeed his father in many of his business and philanthropic pursuits.

Oil from Roosevelt's administration a bitter insult. They should not have been surprised. Roosevelt had coined the term "muckraker" for those journalists who attacked corporations. Roosevelt was not against business, even big business, but he was against what he called "malefactors of great wealth." He argued that such concentrations of wealth and power had to be countered with an equally strong government that could regulate corporations for the good of the entire country. He quickly earned a reputation as an enemy of the trusts.

Roosevelt had many enemies within his own party who were opposed to his reforming agenda. After he was elected governor of New York, the Republican leaders in his home state wanted to find a way to remove him from the office. They hit upon the strategy of making him William McKinley's vice president. What harm could he do in the relatively powerless office of vice president?

Their plan backfired, however, when President McKinley was assassinated in 1901, only months into his second term. Now the reformer and critic of the trusts was president of the United States.

Roosevelt's decision to go after Standard Oil was aided by the publication of Tarbell's series in *McClure's Magazine*. As each installment painted a darker picture of the company, he could sense that public hatred and fear were peaking. Public sentiment was primed for legal action against Standard Oil.

Roosevelt did not focus all his attention on Standard

Oil. He pushed through the Pure Food and Drug Act that sought to regulate the quality of food and medicine. He gave more power to the Interstate Commerce Commission, which had been formed years before but had been rendered ineffective by Congress. He encouraged the commission to regulate railroad rates and to end the types of abuse that had given the oil trust such an advantage.

Roosevelt began his investigation of Standard Oil in 1904. He was not influenced by a contribution Standard Oil made to his campaign, or by Archbold and Rogers's plea not to proceed against the company. After meeting with Roosevelt, Archbold reported back that the president "professed great ignorance of the affairs of the company . . . He exhibited no personal animosity or unkindly feeling." Archbold hoped that he had deterred the president from pursuing an antitrust case against Standard Oil. He was wrong.

On November 18, 1906, in the Federal Circuit Court in St. Louis, the Roosevelt Administration filed suit to dissolve Standard Oil. The federal government charged Standard with conspiring to restrain trade, thus violating the Sherman Antitrust Act of 1890. The federal charges were soon followed by a tidal wave of indictments from state courts. After years of protection, trusts were now under attack from the courts and political leaders—and the oil trust was the top target.

It was the case in St. Louis that posed the greatest threat, however. The government sought to prove that by the use of rebates and price fixing, Standard Oil had sought to destroy any refiners of crude oil and distributors of petroleum products. The trial lasted two years, called 444 witnesses, presented 1371 exhibitions, and filled a transcript of 14,495 pages. Rockefeller himself was called to testify, but he was able to deflect the prosecutor's questions. Despite his performance, however, the court found Standard in violation of the Sherman Antitrust Act and ordered the company to be broken up. By the time the decision was rendered on May 15, 1911, Roosevelt was out of office. He received the news in Africa, where he was on a safari. He exulted in the win and cabled home his congratulations to the federal attorneys.

The decision was appealed to the Supreme Court, where, two years later, the highest Court upheld the verdict. Its decision said that restraint of trade must be reasonable and not work against the public interest. Chief Justice Edward White read: "No disinterested mind can survey the period (since 1870) without being irresistibly drawn to the conclusion that the very genius for commercial development and organization . . . soon begat an intent and purpose to exclude others . . . from their right to trade . . ."

The unexpected, completely shocking element in the decision was that the justices decreed that Standard Oil must be dissolved within six months. Standard executives had to divide the extraordinarily complex and vast company without devaluing the redistributed stock. By

This 1905 political cartoon, titled "Painful Incident of the Cold Spell," shows Rockefeller as a woman at a stove who is being blown away by angry Kansas oil competitors.

July, the executives announced their restructure plans.

Standard Oil was divided into seven companies. Standard Oil of New Jersey was the largest new company, with half the total net value; it eventually became Exxon. Standard Oil of New York had nine percent of net value; it later turned into Mobil. Standard Oil of California in time became Chevron. Standard Oil of Ohio later turned into Soho. Standard Oil of Indiana is now called Amoco. Continental Oil became Conoco. Atlantic Oil turned into ARCO and Sun.

The ironic aspect of the breakup of Standard Oil was that it happened at a perfect time. With the advent of the automobile, the old top-heavy organization would not have been flexible enough to respond to the new opportunities. Now the new, young executives would not have to pay undue homage to the company headquarters at 26 Broadway. They would not have to get permission for capital expenditures over $5000, as they had in the past.

A perfect example is the work of William Burton, the head chemist for Standard of Indiana. Foreseeing that automobiles would increase the need for gasoline, he determined in 1909 to get more gasoline from oil by "cracking," or breaking down, hydrocarbon molecules in other oil products. He experimented with high pressure and high temperatures up to 650° F. The refinery technicians were frightened that he was going to cause an explosion and refused to work. Burton and his chemists ended up carrying out the dangerous experiments alone.

They proved to be successful and provided a tremendous breakthrough for technology.

But when Burton applied for $1 million to ramp up for the increased output of gasoline, the men at 26 Broadway refused. In 1911, the executives at the newly independent Standard of Indiana agreed—and just in time. Henry Ford's Model T was coming off the assembly line, creating a great demand for gasoline. Price per gallon was going up everywhere. From 1911 to 1913, it went from nine to seventeen cents, and in London and Paris drivers paid fifty cents. Elsewhere in Europe it was one dollar.

Standard of Indiana then licensed Burton's thermal cracking process to other companies. The young executives refused to give Standard of New Jersey any of the profits from the cracking process, although they had once been partners in the trust. They chuckled to hear that the president of Standard of New Jersey disliked writing those royalty checks each month to Standard of Indiana.

Shareholders of Standard Oil were reissued stock in all the new companies determined by the restructure percentage rates. Those who did not then sell became even richer, for many doubled or tripled in value. Among the winners was John D. Rockefeller, who believed in Standard Oil, united or divided. The combination of the extra value of the new shares and the explosion of gasoline sales meant that he was now making more money than ever. Although he had been retired for almost two decades, the system he had created now made him the wealthiest man in the world.

Chapter Nine

The Rockefeller Foundation and Other Philanthropies

While the American courts were processing the break up of the Standard Oil Trust, the Rockefeller philanthropies were not put on hold. Although his boss did not gain any relief from the unrelenting negative press by his good deeds, Frederick Gates continued to make judgments about worthy causes and to follow through with large amounts of money. The basic principle guiding his decisions was to try to eliminate the root causes of poverty and ignorance.

The southern United States became a major beneficiary. Still suffering from conditions created by the Civil War fifty years earlier, many Southerners, both black and white, suffered from abysmal living conditions. The Jim Crow laws that ordered racial segregation of public facilities and schools maintained an ugly social mentality that worked to the detriment of poor people of all races.

There were very few public high schools and none at all for blacks in the region. With Junior sharing the lead with Gates, the General Education Board was founded in

1902 for "the promotion of education within the United States without distinction of race, sex, or creed." Rockefeller promised $1 million to be dispensed over ten years.

At first, money went to pay university professors for field work to determine where the high schools should be and which communities would be willing to tax themselves to help start and maintain the schools. By 1910, there were 800 new high schools in the South that Rockefeller's money stimulated.

Rockefeller, Gates, and Junior were disappointed that the distribution ended up going more to help whites than blacks. But there were racists everywhere who stymied help to blacks however they could. From the other side, the African-American leader W. E. B. Du Bois criticized the General Education Board for not fighting school segregation.

In 1906, Gates took Rockefeller's "root out the cause of poverty" one step further. He saw the boll-weevil ruining cotton crops and destroying farmers. Gates connected with Dr. Seaman Knapp of the U.S. Department of Agriculture. This scientist had developed methods of seed selection and farming to eliminate the boll-weevil. He needed money to start demonstration farms in infected areas. The General Education Board made regular contributions to the Department of Agriculture for this and other specific projects. Thus, it is estimated that more than 100,000 farms were improved by 1912. Their prosperity enabled farmers to pay taxes that would support education and other aspects of public well being. This was a perfect example of how Rockefeller wanted his money to empower others.

Another scourge of the South was the hookworm, a parasite that entered the body through the soles of the feet. Many poor Southerners who went barefoot in the summer had no idea that the lack of energy many felt was not caused by anemia, malaria, or hot weather. It was caused by the hookworm that sapped nutrients necessary for growth and health from the body.

In 1902, Dr. Charles W. Stiles, a zoologist, discovered how the hookworm destroyed the human body. He also knew that hookworms were easily eliminated from the body if the infected person drank an extract called *thymol* made from the common herb thyme. Thymol made the hookworms detach themselves from the walls of the intestines, where as many as 5000 might live. When the person then drank Epsom salts, the hookworms were flushed out entirely.

Dr. Stiles was very excited about his discovery and immediately tried to get a program started to banish hookworms forever. His simple solution was also very cheap: The dose of thymol and Epsom salts cost about fifty cents per person. But, much to his surprise, he was not believed. Southerners felt he was insulting them and implying they lived primitively.

For nine years, Stiles tried to get his program enacted.

Finally, he met Frederick Gates and Simon Flexner, who headed the Rockefeller Institute for Medical Research in New York City. They immediately recognized the magnitude of Stiles's cure. It would cost about $1 million to cure the two million afflicted people.

They found the tactful and gracious Wickliffe Rose, dean of the University of Nashville, to head the task force, which they called the U.S. Sanitary Commission, to save the South from the stigma of being singled out. They also had to work against rumors about Rockefeller. Some believed that Rockefeller had invented the "hookworm scheme" after investing in shoe factories as a way to increase sales.

Rockefeller's money paid new doctors through state medical boards to educate people in the areas rife with hookworm. The doctors showed their patients live worms and eggs and before-and-after pictures of afflicted people. Those who underwent the quick cure felt immediate results. Participation in the program snowballed, and when it was over, one scientist judged it to be "the most effective campaign against a widespread disabling disease which medical science and philanthropy have ever combined to conduct." The hookworm was reduced to a treatable affliction. Follow-up treatments were arranged, as was a campaign to fight hookworms in other countries.

The good results achieved through the General Education Board and the Rockefeller Institute for Medical Research certainly assured Rockefeller that he was helping people according to his Baptist principles. He was also very much aware of what more he could do, for his vast wealth was expanding. One projection made in 1906 showed that Rockefeller would be worth $90 billion by 1936, if he only let his money sit and collect interest!

Frederick Gates, having managed Rockefeller's charities for some fifteen years, encouraged him like an old revival style preacher exhorting goodness: "Your fortune is rolling up, rolling up like an avalanche! You must keep up with it! You must distribute it faster than it grows! If you do not, it will crush you and your children and your children's children." Gates was preaching to the converted. Rockefeller had already conceived of a benevolent trust, similar in structure to the trust he established in the corporate world. In 1901, he began calling this philanthropic trust a *foundation*.

Setting up the Rockefeller Foundation was not as easy as it might seem, given the anti-Rockefeller climate in the country. The articles of Ida Tarbell and others had created a personal image of him as an icy monster whose sudden loss of hair, due to a nervous disorder called *alopecia*, was a punishment from God. To these Rockefeller-haters, it looked as if the foundation were merely a ploy to influence the antitrust case then playing out in the courts. Attorney General George Wickersham was shocked by the very notion of the foundation and protested to President Taft the impropriety of Congress granting a charter to a man whose "great combination of wealth" was under legal attack.

Even the goal of the Rockefeller Foundation was suspected. The motto "To promote the well being of mankind throughout the world" was purposefully left vague to allow future boards freedom to give the money where they thought it was needed. But it was interpreted by many as a subterfuge by the crafty Rockefeller to somehow make more money.

Finally, in 1913, the Rockefeller Foundation was chartered in New York by the state legislature. Rockefeller contributed $100 million in the first year. By 1919, he had added almost $83 million more. Before his death in 1937, he gave another $180 million.

Before the Rockefeller Foundation existed, he had already spent $157 million for his various benefactions. Junior would eventually give nearly $1 billion more, either directly or through other philanthropies. Thus, Rockefeller far surpassed the less controversial Andrew Carnegie and his donations of $350 million, becoming the most generous philanthropist in American history.

Eventually, Junior became the president of the Rockefeller Foundation. Frederick Gates wanted to retire and serve as one of the nine trustees. Rockefeller himself was a trustee but did not attend meetings. He was glad to see his son assuming leadership.

Junior and his board tended to favor medical research and public health projects. Very sensitive to the family image, Junior explained that he wanted to avoid the arts and social sciences because they were more subjective and easily pinched political nerves. Medicine, he felt, was a field in which there was much less chance for controversy. Causes and effects could be made clear.

Wickliffe Rose, who headed the hookworm cure in the South, was funded to do the same on a global scale through the new International Health Commission. Rose also headed a campaign against malaria. Scientists paid by the Rockefeller Foundation developed a vaccine for the disease by 1937, saving many lives. Money was also given to create schools of hygiene and public health, first at Harvard and Johns Hopkins Universities and then in cities around the world. At these schools, the students learned about sanitary engineering, epidemiology, and biostatistics.

After the United States, China was the country that benefitted most from the Rockefeller Foundation. The China Medical Board was created in 1915. It built the Peking Union Medical College in 1921. Called the Green City, it had fifty-nine buildings with jade-green tile roofs. It introduced Chinese doctors to the contemporary research and medicine of the West.

By the 1920s, the Rockefeller Foundation was the largest of its kind. The amount of money that Rockefeller had both amassed and given away was by then far less likely to be matched by another man. Antitrust laws, the 1913 passage of the Sixteenth Amendment, (which allowed a federal income tax) and the more restrictive laws passed to control the unlimited accumulation of capital,

Frederick T. Gates was Rockefeller's trusted philanthropic chief.

meant that no other capitalist would work in such a limitless environment. It is not surprising that Rockefeller did not approve of the income tax or other government interventions into the economy. "When a man has accumulated a sum of money, accumulated it within the law, the Government has no right to share in its earnings," he said in 1914.

Chapter Ten

Persistence and Vision

During the same year that the U.S. Supreme Court upheld the division of Standard Oil, another grim event undercut the Rockefeller name. While the so-called "Ludlow Massacre" revealed the negative attitude of Rockefeller toward labor unions, it also demonstrated how Junior was more flexible than his father.

The story began in 1902, when Rockefeller bought a company called Colorado Fuel and Iron (CFI). Frederick Gates advised him to buy the company with money made from the Mesabi iron ore fields in Minnesota. Gates also recommended that his uncle, LaMont Bowers, be named a vice president. He was supposed to keep Gates and Rockefeller informed of how the company was being managed.

Bowers seemed a good candidate because he had successfully run Rockefeller's iron ore fleet on the Great Lakes. What neither Bowers, Gates, nor Rockefeller knew was that the managers of CFI, who were still running the company, were corrupt. In fact, evidence came to light later that Gates had actually been tricked into assuming otherwise.

As bad luck would have it, Junior decided to stay on the CFI corporate board when he resigned from Standard Oil and other Rockefeller business interests in 1910 to focus on the Rockefeller Foundation. Since CFI was not making money, Junior wanted to remain and prove to his father that he could make it profitable. The next few years would turn out to be the most bitter of his public life.

CFI was no small company. It ran twenty-four mines and was the largest employer in Colorado. It was the second-largest steel company in the U.S. Junior was puzzled by its inability to show a profit and was plodding through its accounts when an explosion killed seventy-nine miners on January 13, 1910.

Bowers reported that the explosion resulted from the miners' carelessness. But the Colorado Bureau of Labor Statistics officials judged otherwise. They knew how dangerous mining was, with several hundred men killed each year, and how dismal life was for the miners, the processing plant workers, and their families. They had to buy from company stores. Armed men were often hired to scare them to work when the conditions were especially dangerous. Soot and mud were everywhere.

Union leaders began organizing at the company. It proved to be fertile ground for recruitment because conditions clearly needed to be bettered and the workers given more control of their security. The United Mine

Workers (UMW) sent in experienced agents and advised the workers to strike. At the same time, Bowers lied, writing to Junior that the workers were happy and satisfied. Instead of going to Colorado to see the conditions himself, Junior trusted Bowers's report. As the workers began agitating, Junior adopted his father's policy of not acknowledging the union's legitimacy and refused to negotiate with it.

John D. Rockefeller saw unions as having the potential to ruin not only his companies, but all private enterprise. He considered himself to be the first domino under pressure: If he gave in, the whole line would necessarily fall. He believed that anyone who wanted to make more money could do what he had done and start a business. He thought workers could not handle the higher wages and would only use them in sinful activities such as card games, plays, dancing, and drinking. He concluded, "Soon the real object of their organizing shows itself—to do as little as possible for the greatest possible pay."

President Woodrow Wilson and his Secretary of Labor were concerned about the Colorado situation. They heard that gunmen had been hired through a detective agency and that these gunmen had been deputized. This meant the mine officials had the force of the law working for them. They also had an armored car with machine guns attached. The Secretary of Labor sent an emissary to Junior, but he referred him to Bowers, who, he said, was on the scene and really knew what was going on.

Demanding a union, better wages, lower hours, and better housing, 9000 workers at CFI went on strike on September 26, 1913. The strikers were then evicted from their company-owned homes. They built tent towns, one of which they called Ludlow. The number of strikers increased to 11,000 in a few days. The angry workers and their families lived uncomfortably in makeshift conditions surrounded by armed men.

On October 17, a gun battle flared. The deputies swooped in with their armored car loaded with machine guns and strafed the tent town, killing several men. But a worse toll was taken by the terrible Rocky Mountain winter as the tent dwellers died of disease and exposure. The efforts by President Wilson and the governor of Colorado to create an agreement produced nothing. Bowers continued to send false reports east to Junior.

In late April 1914, another gun battle ignited. The Colorado militiamen sent by the governor to aid the company not only shot viciously into the tents, but set the tents on fire. Two women and eleven children huddling in a dirt trench died of smoke inhalation as the fire swept over them.

Junior issued a statement denying blame on the part of the company. He based his statement on the inaccurate information supplied by Bowers. Newspapers all over the country soon told quite another story. The image of the grasping, deceitful, win-at-all-costs Rockefeller created by Tarbell seemed once again justified.

Angry protests flared up outside the Rockefeller homes. The family had to fortify their estates, hire guards, and watch their backs in public. Rockefeller could see it no other way than that he was right and the strikers wrong. But Junior saw the larger picture. He did not want to hurt his father, but he saw that company policy toward unions and strikes must change. *How?* was the dilemma for him.

Mackenzie King helped him make this change without dishonoring his father. King had been a Canadian minister of labor. He joined the Rockefeller Foundation as an economic-research adviser. He believed in collective bargaining between owners and unions and had proven effective as an arbitrator in Canadian labor disputes.

King and Junior liked each other instantly. King intuited that Junior truly wanted to do good. He wanted to reconcile the needs of the strikers with his strong love of his father and sense of duty. King convinced him that secrecy and stonewalling were methods of the past. One must now "take the public into one's confidence, to give publicity to many things, and especially to stand out for certain principles very broadly."

The first step in Colorado, King urged, was to provide the workers with an elected representation within the company. Union organizers denounced this as paternalism, and CFI officials thought it was capitulating to the strikers. But Rockefeller praised his son and expressed pride that he was trying a tactic that he himself would never have attempted.

By January 1915, Junior was testifying humbly and openly at the U.S. Commission on Industrial Relations in New York City. Although he had been warned of possible trouble, he refused to sneak in the rear door. He shook hands with union organizers from Colorado and even invited Mother Jones, the most famous organizer, to his office. He did what was unthinkable for his father: He apologized publicly for being narrow and misinformed about the events at the Colorado mines.

Family deaths—his mother's and his father-in-law's—prevented Junior from traveling immediately to Colorado. But by September he was standing in the former tent town of Ludlow and visiting with the miners, who were now back to work. He even danced with the miners' wives that evening. In Pueblo, he presented to CFI workers and managers his proposition for grievance committees, better working conditions, and new benefits.

He promised that no one would be fired for joining a union. In 1933, the United Mine Workers finally did succeed in organizing the Ludlow miners. Junior's "company union" was made illegal by the Wagner Act of 1935.

Junior's new principles regarding labor relations were evident later in plans for employee representation devised at the various Standard Oil companies. In 1920, he sold his stock in U.S. Steel when the company refused to meet the demands of strikers to shorten work hours. During the Great Depression of the 1930s, Junior undertook the creation of Rockefeller Center in midtown Manhattan.

The soaring buildings of steel, limestone, and glass with art deco surface detail gave work to 75,000 unionized construction workers.

The events in Colorado and elsewhere in his vast empire had little impact on John D. Rockefeller's daily life. All his life, John D. Rockefeller exercised the character qualities that defined him: persistence, foresight, subtlety of mind, love of system, and keen curiosity in all practical affairs. He wanted to live to be 100 years old, and he planned carefully how to do it. He gradually retired, and by 1906, he was starting to enjoy it.

The social element in his personality bloomed during retirement. He talked to everyone—farmers in the fields he drove by, train passengers traveling with him, the children of his employees. He loved jokes and stories. His quips show his alert, humorous mind. Once, with a twinkle in his eyes, he excused himself to a visitor by saying he had "to get to work and see if I can do something to keep the wolf away from the door!"

He maintained a regular daily schedule. He rose about 6 A.M. and took time to read the newspaper and stroll the garden paths he designed for his homes. He allowed digestion time after his fairly simple meals and took naps. He worked on his mail and reviewed business updates regarding his philanthropies and investments. He played golf and mind games such as Numerica. Replacing the horseback riding or carriage driving that he had thoroughly loved in his younger days, as an older person

Rockefeller liked to be chauffeured in a car around his estate in the afternoons. In the evenings, he liked to entertain guests for dinner and listen to music afterwards. His Baptist lifestyle never allowed alcohol, tobacco, dancing, or cards, but he did attend a few plays later in life.

Rockefeller developed a seasonal schedule as well. He and Cettie spent their summers at Forest Hill outside Cleveland. Then they returned to their New York City residence at Four West Fifty-fourth Street or to the large Pocantico Hills estate above the Hudson River. As his love for golf grew, he added several homes with golf courses—one at Lakewood, New Jersey, and the other at Ormond Beach, Florida, where he spent a winter season that he extended as he aged. He testified in court—when he could not avoid it—regarding the antitrust lawsuit or collusion with railroads.

Rockefeller remained devoted and loving to Cettie. But whereas Rockefeller was active in mind and body as he aged, Cettie limited her interests and shrunk her range of activity. The lively, inquiring college girl in Massachusetts and teacher in Cleveland turned into a religious devotee. She was a strict and thrifty mother who valued self-denial for herself and tried to teach it to her children. Once when Junior disclosed what he wanted for Christmas, she told a friend how pleased she was to find out because now she could deny him that and thus strengthen his character. The moral formation of her children was her chief goal. She believed home was the best place for her children to learn during their grade school years. Only at home could she direct their tutors and oversee their prayers and moral self-examinations.

Cettie's physical ailments multiplied over the years. By 1909, she confined herself to a bed or wheelchair and relied on full-time nurses. Her diary describes illnesses including pneumonia, shingles, anemia, and sciatica. Rockefeller remained faithful, even romantic, to her. On their fiftieth wedding anniversary in 1914, he hired a band to play Mendelssohn's "Wedding March" while she was carried out to the lawn at Pocantico Hills.

Cettie died in 1915 and was buried in the family plot in Cleveland's Lake View Cemetery. Rockefeller's final tribute to her was the $74 million Laura Spelman Rockefeller Memorial Foundation. It funded social science research and eventually became part of the Rockefeller Foundation.

In addition to running the Rockefeller Foundation, Junior also wanted to promote public life. Visitors to the restored eighteenth-century colonial capital of Williamsburg, Virginia, have Junior to thank. He also donated a fabulous collection of medieval art to The Cloisters museum in Manhattan. As he did not share his wife Abby's enthusiasm for modern art, she independently co-founded the Museum of Modern Art, also in Manhattan. In time, the two Rockefeller town houses on Fifty-fourth Street were razed to provide land for the museum.

The credit for Rockefeller Center in midtown Manhattan also goes to Junior. Though the project was laughed at by many at first, he carried through with it despite the blows to his fortune from the Crash of 1929 and the Great Depression. Standard Oil moved to the building from the old headquarters at 26 Broadway. Junior ceremoniously hammered in the last rivet in 1939.

A beautiful example of art deco architecture, Rockefeller Center remains a major architectural feature of New York City. J. D. Salinger's 1950 novel *The Catcher in the Rye* depicts sixteen-year-old Holden Caulfield seeing a movie and a live Christmas show at Radio City. He later ice skates with Sally Hayes on the ice rink in front of the Center.

Junior also contributed to the quality of American lives in more natural settings. The John D. Rockefeller, Jr. National Highway takes cars past the Grand Teton mountains to Yellowstone National Park. After the Rockefellers visited there several times, they were appalled by the litter and ugly commercial trappings. Junior bought up land around Jackson Hole and gave it to the National Parks. He also gave preservation money to Yosemite, the California redwoods, the Shenandoah and Great Smoky National Parks, and to the Hudson River Palisades Park.

Junior set up trusts for his family totaling $102 million. Between 1917 and 1960, he donated $537 million directly and another $540 million through the Rockefeller philanthropies.

A stately John D. Rockefeller, 1910.

As his son moved on the public stage, Rockefeller enjoyed his private life of golf and visits with his grandchildren. At age ninety-five, he moved permanently to The Casements in Ormond, Florida. He had to give up golf after the move, but he exercised on a stationary bicycle. He enjoyed movies, singing, and afternoon car rides with a few friends. On the day he died, he paid off the mortgage on the Euclid Avenue Baptist Church in Cleveland.

John D. Rockefeller did not make his goal of living to 100. He was nearly ninety-eight when he died in his sleep on May 23, 1937, after a heart attack. His body was taken by train for a funeral at Pocantico Hills, New York, and then on to Cleveland for burial in the plot with his mother, Eliza, on one side and his wife, Cettie, on the other. To thwart future vandals, his tomb was made bombproof with heavy stone. With most of his money contributed already to philanthropy, Rockefeller's personal estate was valued at only $26 million.

The judgment on Rockefeller has varied from villain to hero since his own day, but all agree on his tremendous influence. He carried out the industrial trust and the philanthropic trust on a scale of magnitude and efficiency that continues to influence the world.

Glossary

---

cartel: An association of businessmen organized to create a national or international monopoly by setting prices and controlling production; a business trust.

consensus: The process in group decision-making of compromising and refining until all can agree.

double entry bookkeeping: System of accounting in which every transaction is entered both as a debit and a credit. The total debits should equal the total credits. It has been called by economic historians "the towering monument" to rational cost-profit calculations.

drawback: Money taken from the total paid to a shipper by regular rates and given to bigger customers as a "bonus" or "overcharge" to keep their business. Historian Allan Nevins says, "Of all the devices for the extinction of competition, this was the cruelest and most deadly yet conceived by any group of American industrialists." Standard Oil as a member of the South Improvement Company, for example, got a rebate of forty cents from the railroad for transporting a barrel of crude oil to Cleveland, *and* it got forty cents for every barrel shipped to Cleveland by competitors.

eminent domain: Legal term for the government's right to take private property for public use after showing the need and paying the owner a fair price.

holding company: A corporation specifically created to hold stocks or bonds for other corporations, which it usually controls.

kerosene: (from the Greek *keros*, wax + *elaion*, oil) A thin oil refined from crude oil used for lamps and fuel.

oil refining: "Cleansing" crude oil with sulfuric acid to turn it into oil products. The refining done in Rockefeller's early refinery has been described as fairly simple and cheap, essentially a process of cooking combined with a few chemicals for purification: Crude oil was strained from wooden troughs into a wood tank, then emptied into a "still" to be boiled. One part of the oil rose as vapor into overhead pipes and was there cooled or condensed into a bluish-white liquid called distillate. This was conveyed into tanks of water heated just below the boiling point; as it rose through the water to the top, a waste vapor was generated and carried away, while the remainder of the distillate was piped off to a tank called the agitator. Here it was mixed thoroughly with sulfuric acid, which combined with the pitch that held it in suspension. The distillate was thus sweetened or purified; the acid and pitch sank to the bottom in a tarry combination known as sludge, while the oil was ready for further cleansing. This was received by a new water bath and the application of a solution of caustic soda to give it brilliancy, after which it was drawn into settling tanks. It was then barreled as refined oil or kerosene.

monopoly: (from the Greek *mono,* one + *polein,* sell) complete control of a kind of goods or service by eliminating all competitors.

muckraker: In a 1906 speech, Theodore Roosevelt referred to the Man with the Muckrake, a character in *Pilgrim's Progress*, to describe a person charging individuals, corporations, or government with corruption. The term can have a negative implication, meaning a person who unfairly or too dramatically makes charges of misconduct.

Numerica: A game in which small square counters are used to try to build four stacks of consecutive numbers from 1 to 13.

petroleum: Another name for *oil*, from the Greek *petra*, rock + *oleum*, oil.

philanthropy: (from the Greek *philein*, to love + *anthropos*, man, humankind) Love for the human race shown through large, usually monetary gifts to institutions for welfare and culture.

rebate: 1) A part of a bill given back to the buyer; this is what it means today. If a car manufacturer advertises "a $1000 rebate," the customer pays the dealer his asking price and then sends his receipt to the manufacturer who mails him a rebate check for $1000. **2)** A discount or deduction on a bill. This is the meaning in Rockefeller's dealings. The rebates were secret agreements between railroads and businessmen that deviated from the published rates.

How ethical this practice was is "the very root of any judgment upon Rockefeller's business methods," says historian Allan Nevins. The practice was common where railroads were very competitive with each other. Rockefeller's view was that a firm with large, regular shipments should be entitled to more consideration than the small, irregular customer.

After unsuccessful efforts to outlaw rebates in individual states, they were forbidden by the Interstate Commerce Act of 1887, which created a commission with power to set rates. The Elkins Act of 1903 and the Hepburn

Act of 1906 enforced the law and discouraged further abuses.

trust: A combination of businesses in which control is given to a single board of trustees who try to control the market by setting prices, eliminating competition, etc.

vertical integration: Control of all aspects of production, sales, and delivery in a given industry.

Timeline

1839—John D. Rockefeller born May 23, Richford, New York, to Eliza Davison and William Avery Rockefeller.

1843—Family moves to Moravia, New York.

1850—Family moves to Owego, New York.

1853—Family moves to Cleveland area. JDR and William attend Central High School, Cleveland.

1854—Baptism at Erie Street Baptist Mission Church, Cleveland.

1855—First job: bookkeeper for Hewitt & Tuttle wholesale produce shippers.

1859—Clark & Rockefeller Produce founded.

1863—Andrews, Clark and Company oil refining begun.

1865—Rockefeller buys out Clark for $72,500, thus beginning the modern oil industry with Rockefeller & Andrews Excelsior Oil Works.

1870—Standard Oil of Ohio, capitalized at $1 million.

1872—South Improvement Company created. The plan, launched by railroads to guarantee each oil-carrying line business and offer greatly reduced rates to member refiners, including Standard, infuriates crude oil producers, who publicize and "kill" it.

1879—Standard Oil controls ninety percent of U.S. oil-refining capacity.

1881—Henry Demarest Lloyd's series, "The Story of a Great Monopoly" in the *Atlantic Monthly*.

1882—Standard Oil trust created, considered the first modern trust in American business history with nine-member board of trustees.

1887—Interstate Commerce Act prohibits discriminatory rates and practices in interstate shipping.

1890—Sherman Antitrust Act prohibits interstate restraint of free trade.

1891—Frederick Gates oversees Rockefeller philanthropies.

1890s—Rockefeller suffers severe stress and delegates more management to John Archbold by 1897.

1892—University of Chicago founded, William Rainey Harper president.

1899—Standard Oil of New Jersey chartered as a holding company with $110 million capitalization for all Standard Oil stock.

1901—Rockefeller Institute for Medical Research founded, New York City.

1902—General Education Board founded for educational and research projects.

1902-05—Ida Tarbell's twenty-four negative articles on

Standard Oil and John D. Rockefeller appear in *McClure's Magazine*.

1905—U.S. House of Representatives antitrust investigation of Standard Oil.

1906-08—Federal prosecution; Standard Oil found guilty and ordered to dissolve; lawyers appeal decision.

1911—U.S. Supreme Court orders holding company dissolved and directors to relinquish control over the subsidiaries within six months.

1913—Rockefeller Foundation established to promote public health and to further medical, natural, and social sciences.

1915—Laura Spelman Rockefeller dies, Pocantico Hills, NY.

1918—Laura Spelman Rockefeller Memorial Foundation founded for child welfare and social sciences.

1937—Death of John D. Rockefeller, Ormond Beach, Florida. Lifetime donations through his philanthropies come to $540 million.

Sources

CHAPTER ONE–Family History

p. 13, "You don't think I'm playing to get beaten, do you?" Ron Chernow, *Titan* (New York: Random House, 1998), 18.

p. 14, "We will let it simmer," Ibid., 22.

p. 15, "I was not an easy student . . ." Ibid., 17.

p. 15, "Dr. William A. Rockefeller, the Celebrated Cancer Specialist . . ." Ibid., 38.

p. 17, "There were younger brothers and sisters to educate . . ." Ibid., 43.

p. 17, "I was working every day at my business–the business of looking for work." Ibid., 44.

p. 18, "No one wanted a boy . . ." Ibid., 45.

CHAPTER TWO–Smart Young Businessman

p. 20, "all the method and system of the office." Chernow, *Titan*, 46.

p. 21, "The zest of the work is maintained by something better than the mere accumulation of money." Ibid., 48

p. 23, " 'We are engaged in business,' I would say," Allan Nevins, *John D. Rockefeller: The Heroic Age of American Enterprise.* Vol. I (New York: Charles Scribner's Sons, 1940), 135.

CHAPTER THREE–The New Oil Industry

p. 34, "I'll go no higher, John." Chernow, *Titan*, 87.

p. 36, "Young man, you can have all the money you want . . ." Ibid., 108.

p. 36, "A friendship founded on business is better . . ." Ibid., 109.

CHAPTER FOUR–Standard Oil Company

p. 48, "I remember a night when my father came home with a grim look on his face . . ." Ida Tarbell, *All in the Days Work: An Autobiography*, (New York: Macmillan, 1939), 23-24.

p. 48, "There was never a shipment made or a rebate or drawback collected . . ." Chernow, *Titan*, 142.

p. 50, "Success comes from . . ." Ibid., 174.

CHAPTER FIVE–The Trust

p. 51, "I believe it is my duty to make money . . ." Chernow, *Titan*, 153.

CHAPTER SIX–The Philanthropist Emerges

p. 68, "You are getting together a lot of scribblers," Chernow, *Titan*, 326.

p. 69, "There is no useless knowledge in medical research . . ." Ibid., 474.

CHAPTER SEVEN–Whipping Time

p. 71, "Whew! It's an expensive house, isn't it?" Chernow, *Titan*, 161.

p. 71, "How many drops of solder do you use in each can?" Ibid., 180.

p. 74, "ought to be in the penitentiary." Ibid., 340.
p. 76, "systematically played with loaded dice." Ida Tarbell, *The History of the Standard Oil Company,* Vol. II, (Gloucester, MA: Peter Smith, 1904), 287.
p. 78, "a living mummy . . . hypocritical facade . . ." Chernow, *Titan,* 453.
p. 78, "Miss Tar Barrell" Ibid., 457.

CHAPTER EIGHT–Break Up
p. 85, ". . .professed great ignorance," Chernow, *Titan ,* 521.
p. 86, "No disinterested mind can survey the period (since 1870) without being irresistibly drawn . . ." Chernow, *Titan,* 554.

CHAPTER NINE–The Rockefeller Foundation . . .
p. 91, "the promotion of education within the United States . . ." Chernow, *Titan,* 484.
p. 93, "the most effective campaign against a widespread disabling disease . . ." Ibid., 491.
p. 94, "Your fortune is rolling up, rolling up like an avalanche!" Ibid., 563.
p. 98, "When a man has accumulated a sum of money, accumulated it within the law . . ." Ibid., 566.

CHAPTER TEN–Persistence and Vision
p. 101, "Soon the real object of their organizing shows itself . . ." Chernow, *Titan,* 574.
p. 103, "take the public into one's confidence, to give publicity to many things . . ." H. M. Gitleman, *Legacy of the Ludlow Massacre: A Chapter in American Industrial Relations,* (Philadelphia: University of PA Press, 1988), 64.

p. 105, "to get to work and see if I can do something to keep the wolf away . . ." Peter Collier and David Horowitz, *The Rockefellers: An American Dynasty*, (New York: Holt, Rhinehart and Winston, 1976), 172.

Bibliography

Chernow, Ron. *Titan*. New York: Random House, 1998.

Manchester, William. *A Rockefeller Family Portrait from John D. to Nelson.* Boston: Little, Brown, 1959.

Nevins, Allan. *John D. Rockefeller: The Heroic Age of American Enterprise.* Two Vols. New York: Charles Scribner's Sons, 1940.

Rockefeller, John D. *Random Reminiscences of Men and Events,* 1909. Tarrytown, New York: Sleepy Hollow Press, 1948.

"Rockefeller, John D." *American National Biography.* New York: Oxford Press, 1999.

Yergin, Daniel. *The Prize: The Epic Quest for Oil, Money and Power.* New York: Simon & Schuster, 1991.

Index